IT'S WHAT YOU DO NEXT

The Fall and Rise of Nostalgia's Platismemia Myra

MEGAN EARBY

IT'S
WHAT
YOU
DO
NEXT

IT'S WHAT YOU DO NEXT

The Fall and Rise of Nashville's First Female Mayor

MEGAN BARRY

Matt Holt Books
An Imprint of BenBella Books, Inc.
Dallas, TX

This book is based on the notes and recollections of the author. Some names and other identifying details have been changed or omitted to protect the privacy of individuals. Any resemblance between a fictionalized name and a real person is strictly coincidental. In passages containing dialogue, quotation marks are used when the author is reasonably sure that the speaker's words are close to verbatim and/or that the speaker's intended meaning was accurately reflected.

Matt Holt is an imprint of BenBella Books, Inc.
10440 N. Central Expressway
Suite 800
Dallas, TX 75231
benbellabooks.com
Send feedback to feedback@benbellabooks.com

BenBella and *Matt Holt* are federally registered trademarks.

Printed in the United States of America
10 9 8 7 6 5 4 3 2 1

Library of Congress Control Number: 2024019311
ISBN 9781637744949 (hardcover)
ISBN 9781637744956 (electronic)

Editing by Katie Dickman
Copyediting by Jennifer Brett Greenstein
Proofreading by Marissa Wold Uhrina and Ashley Casteel
Text design and composition by PerfecType, Nashville, TN
Cover design by Brigid Pearson
Cover photograph by CJ Hicks
Printed by Lake Book Manufacturing

Special discounts for bulk sales are available. Please contact bulkorders@benbellabooks.com.

For Bruce and Max, the two people I love the most

CONTENTS

AUTHOR'S NOTE

Truth Is the First Casualty of Memoir

My husband and I had a conversation about the book yesterday.

"Apparently, the first casualty of memoir is truth," Bruce says after reading my first draft. "You make me sound like a huge ass."

He's not an ass. But he's not a teddy bear either. We're out back having a drink, something we make a point of doing often because it's good for a marriage and because the azaleas are in full bloom.

"This is *my* truth. It's how I remember things," I argue (but softly). "Consider yourself a character in the story, one who the reader has to see the flaws in to find the plot."

At this, he rolls his eyes. He's not an ass or a teddy bear *or* a character. He's not a hero or a villain either. Neither of us are.

He takes a sip of his drink. He can't believe I'm giving him a "*my* truth" speech.

"Do you really see me that way? Did you really think I was distant and uncaring and absent?" he asks.

Slowly, I nod. At the time, I did, but my memory is pretty one-sided. I remember me. And that's all this book can profess to remember.

This book is my truth, and I am the biggest ass in this story. My husband and all the others whom I write about have their own memories and accounts. My goal has not been to write this in a way that hurts or harms anyone. I've tried my best to reconstruct how things unfolded. All the rest are memories. You have your memories too.

Depending on where you are in the world, you may have forgotten about me, but it'll probably come back to you as we go. Here are some headlines:

"Megan Barry Resigns as Nashville Mayor, Weeks After Admitting Affair with Her Security Chief" —*Washington Post*
"Megan Barry, Nashville Mayor, Pleads Guilty to Theft and Agrees to Resign" —*New York Times*
"Nashville's Music-Loving Mayor Megan Barry Resigns in Wake of Adultery Scandal" —*Variety*

I was a public servant who became a public scandal, and as glorious and memorable as my rise to office was, the fall was just as spectacular. As the Trump train chugged along, grabbing pussies and taking names, and #MeToo fired back at America's bloated and busted patriarchy, my political career came and went. My story was documented zealously by the press. Some of it, anyway. They only left out the stuff that mattered.

I'm not writing this book for absolution. By the grace of God, my family, my friends, and myself, I have that. I'm writing because at some point, all of us will be at our worst. Some of us will be remembered for it, but none of us should be defined by it. It's what you do next that counts.

Lovingly,
Megan

IT'S WHAT YOU DO NEXT

Class Secretary

Fifth-Grade Elections, Katherine Carpenter Elementary School, 1974

Megan Mueller: 12 votes

Suzie D.: 13 votes

"Why did you vote for Suzie?"

Mom is sitting across from me at the round oak kitchen table, words in one corner of her mouth and a Kool menthol cigarette in the other. Her pink lips pucker around the end of the filter and she thumbs at her lighter, shaking it, flicking it, scowling at it, until it ignites. The murky amber-colored ashtray between us is overflowing with butts. Soot has spilled out onto one of the fancy quilted placemats, frosting a corner in dark residue. I reach over and brush it off, grinding the ash into the woodgrain of the table with the heel of my hand and watching a peel of smoke reach up toward the ceiling, liking how it sways like a cat's tail.

"Megan?"

She leans closer but does not drop her voice. Mom's not trying to scare me, but rather to convey, as she often does, that she doesn't have time to fuck around. I should answer quickly. Dinner is on the stove. In her daily decathlon of homemaking, dinner is the penultimate

1

challenge before bed. She's younger than the other moms at school, but her face is harder. Her lips and eyes are fringed with furrows and stitches that come, I guess, with not having time to fuck around.

I don't know what to say to her. I just ran for class secretary and lost by one vote, my own. In 1974, class secretary is the only thing little girls are allowed to be in fifth-grade politics. Not president or vice president. Title IX is two years old but doesn't seem to have reached Overland Park, Kansas, yet. Michaels and Toms make the decisions; Suzies and Megans record them. In this case, a Suzie.

My chest is tight and sore, like there are elastic bands strung over my rib cage. It never occurred to me that I should write my own name on the ballot, a tiny strip of paper torn from our teacher, Mrs. Patton's, memo pad. Suzie is one of my best friends. I thought voting for her was the right thing to do. And I really thought she would vote for me too.

Shit.

I'm not allowed to say "shit" out loud, but I love the way it sounds in my head.

The fog and sizzle of the kitchen grows thick behind Mom. Sale pork chops hiss in a hot pan. Murmuring in the pot next to it are two cans of Del Monte peas and carrots. She shouts my name again over the sound.

"Megan!"

I hate when she's disappointed in me, so I shrug my shoulders and say nothing, admit to nothing, play it safe. But she knows.

"I was at school earlier today . . ." she starts in. After her regular morning of decoupage and crafting, she had unspooled her hair from its curlers, sealed herself into a girdle, and driven to my elementary school.

Shit.

She waits for me to say something, anything, as she stands up from the table to flip the chops, which scream louder when they hit the skillet. She takes a minute to stare into the cheap meat like it's revealing the future. I stare into her, terrified that she's revealing mine: she's sad, regretful, and married to an unfaithful man who comes in and out of our lives at his convenience while she takes care of everything all day and quietly sews out her rage in the evenings. She hurls a pinch of salt onto the peas. Mom doesn't cook food; it submits to her.

"I counted all the votes for the entire fifth grade," she declares.

She knows my handwriting. She's proud of it—elegant and precise script, thin and full in all the right places, just like hers. No quavering lines, no evidence of indecision. My "Suzie" was as beautiful as it was stupid. Still, I say nothing about it.

"Dad coming home?" I ask, trying to change the subject.

He's not. She counted the votes, and I counted the pork chops. Dad is rarely home for dinner. He owns two restaurants and a bar in town and works long, late hours. When he isn't working, he spends time with his friends: the pilot, the doctor, the piano salesman, the guy he met when he played the role of the train conductor in our local production of *Cabaret*. Mom doesn't like Dad's friends. And she said the set of *Cabaret* looked cheap.

"He's not coming," she shoots back. "Now tell me why you voted for Suzie."

She turns off the burner and begins arranging the pork on a white platter. There's no more dancing around it.

"Suzie's my best friend," I mutter softly, feeling small and foolish. "I wanted to be nice."

"You shouldn't have done that," Mom says with a frown. "Honey, if you don't believe in yourself, nobody else will believe in you either."

She's right. Being nice was a mistake.

Tugboat

It's ringing.

"Megan, she can't hear you smiling."

It's January 2015, and my campaign fundraiser, Brian, is scolding me, tracing the enormous swan-white grin on his face with an index finger and trying to convince me that if I don't "twinkle up," eighty-six-year-old Democrat and lifelong Nashvillian Myrtle Pink isn't going to sense my leadership potential.

If she even answers.

It's still ringing.

I wager that if Myrtle's headed to the phone, she's not breaking any land speed records, so I take a big swig of coffee and let my jaw go slack before re-twinkling, smiling wide and clownlike, until my eyes water. Mercifully, Myrtle answers and gives us a hundred bucks. I hang up and rub my cheeks before practicing my phone smile again.

"There!" Brian marvels. "Just beautiful!"

His smile is better than mine *and* more audible, but he's a twenty-six-year-old genius who looks like a Filipino John Stamos, not a first-time mayoral candidate approaching middle age with no budget to twinkle about. Brian scans his list for the next potential benefactor and sends me a thumbs-up from across the table.

"He's good," Bruce remarks, standing in a beam of morning sun. He's reluctantly awestruck, which is the only way my husband of twenty years approaches a state of wonder. As a couple, we have an unspoken agreement not to "twinkle." At least not in the other's presence.

"I know," I chuckle, "Brian's great. He should probably try out for *American Idol*."

Bruce shrugs and then asks, "Do you think he'd wear one of your buttons on the show?"

We both look down at a shoebox full of enameled "Megan Barry for Mayor" pins and quietly discuss Brian's (probably amazing) singing voice and star power. I settle into the hard-backed chair that makes my butt hurt but keeps my back straight, another trick to keep the charisma fresh and flowing.

"Meggie," Bruce jokes, "don't forget to smile." He grabs his coffee and makes his way down the hall to his office. I hear the door click softly as he retreats into his world.

"Not a chance," I promise behind him.

Together, Brian and I raise $1,600 that day. Every penny counts.

• • •

As a two-term councilwoman, I have the experience to be mayor. I know my way around the Metro Courthouse (Nashville's city hall). I can advocate and collaborate. I've done my time in the Parent Teacher Organization (bring your brass knuckles) and in the neighborhood association (bring a covered dish). I've even done corporate America (bring your spine if you've still got it). Until recently, I worked for a private healthcare company as an ethics and compliance officer, the kind they send around the country from Marriott Courtyard to Marriott Courtyard to remind the C-levels not to download porn on their work computers or engage in conflicts of interest (i.e., affairs). I've done just about everything except pose a legitimate threat to the status quo, which down here, feels impossible without an ace up your sleeve and a Y chromosome in your back pocket. My biggest rival in the mayor's race, Opponent A, doesn't even have enough respect for me to fear me. I'm not sure the rest of the field even knows I'm here.

Right now, the only votes I can count on belong to Bruce and Max, our son, who promises his friends will vote for me too. Depending on what they get up to the night before, I guess.

In the Metro Council, my attempts to push progressive bills have mostly been met with grumbles, but when you're dealing with bureaucrats of a certain age and certain income bracket, grumbles happen. The important thing is that the legislation is passing. I can get shit done. I can get *good* shit done. Times, they are a-changin'.

Nashville is a progressive city in denial. It has been for a while. Or at least, Bruce and I have been talking about it for a while since we first met at Vanderbilt, where he's a professor and I was a graduate student (not his). Our courtship mostly consisted of listening to "Tangled Up in Blue" on his porch and watching Cold War films until 3 AM. (Well, *he* was watching Pudvokin and Klimov; I was trying to keep my eyes open.) But we also discussed, debated, and deconstructed Nashville, the unlikely love of our lives. For all the fire and brimstone at the megachurch, there's as much rock and roll at the mother church of the Grand Ole Opry. For every prayer circle, there's a drum circle. We've got the Tea Party crowd, but we've got the block party crowd too. There are students and musicians, big tech is coming from out west, and new residents are hailing from everywhere—Los Angeles, Kurdistan, El Salvador, Canada. They're bringing their politics with them and electing council members more interested in equality, education, and community wellness than they are in tax cuts. There's less harkening back to the way things were and more imagining the way they could be. And they could be great. There's an electricity here, a thrumming. I have about as much of a shot at bagging this victory as I do Jon Hamm, but if there's a time for me, for us, it's *right now.*

My entire campaign staff is focused on our first televised debate. There are seven of us in a crowded field, all trying to find our lanes and stand out. We've been traipsing the county, all 520 square miles of it, appearing nearly anywhere we're asked to appear. Interested in birding at Percy Warner Park? Let's bird. Having a family reunion? Call me Cousin Meg. If we're asked to show up, we show up. Bonus points if a vague social or political issue comes up. My campaign is low on funds even though Bruce and I took a loan against the house. A televised public forum like this one matters. We can reach more people and spend less gas money.

The auditorium at Belmont University is shockingly full when we arrive. The usual press is here, mostly to see Opponent A, and the rest of the audience is college kids, who I'm sure are getting course credit just for showing up. We all file onstage and try to find faces beyond the too-bright TV lights. I'm wearing a Calvin Klein sheath dress and a smear of blush called Aphrodite. If I'm going to stand half a chance, I'll need a goddess or two to step in.

"The first question is for Megan Barry," the moderator says. He's cheerful and probably too affable to pull this gig off convincingly, more of a Pat Sajak than a Wolf Blitzer.

We've all drawn lots before going onstage to determine the order of the questions. I'm up first and I can already feel the Aphrodite melting off me.

"You'll have one minute to answer the following," the mod chirps.

Fuck. I wasn't expecting them to start so fast.

The stool I'm sitting on wobbles. A bar stool is the lousiest option possible for a short woman in a skirt and Spanx. I peek over and notice that Opponent A, one of several local businessmen, has wisely chosen against his skirt and Spanx today. Plus, I've been talked into wearing higher-than-normal heels. I should have stuck with my comfortable shoes because I'm going to have to stand and lean against the god-awful stool for the entirety of the debate. No way am I going to risk hoisting myself up and flashing the audience, though it sure as hell would be memorable. Instinctively, I cross my legs and stand up straight, Brian-style, at the thought.

"Ma'am?" the mod presses.

I'm so fixated on the stool that I miss the first question completely and look up big-eyed and frozen like a scared rabbit.

"I'm sorry. Can you please repeat the question?" I stammer, trying to look natural with my stool.

The moderator speaks again. This time, I hear him. The question is about infrastructure, and I could answer it in my sleep. I answer coherently and feel my voice reverberate around the egg-shaped room. There's no pomp and circumstance about it. I don't talk like a winner, or even a politician. I talk to the audience like they're my neighbors; after all, that's what they are. I'm too exhausted from being at the back of the pack, and I don't have the energy to put on a show.

And it's working for me.

People are listening. The audience is smiling, or "twinkling," as Brian would say. They start to laugh. They like me. My stool and I appear to be a breath of fresh air, which hell, I'll take. Opponents A and B are petrified on their tall perches and visibly pissed off.

After another forty minutes of questions and answers, I walk off-stage looking like I just got out of a spin class. My blood is pumping. So are my sweat glands. But I nailed it.

My team is standing near the emergency exit looking awkward, like they're all in line for the bathroom. Nobody says anything.

"What do you think?" I ask them, breathless and victorious. "Good?"

"You did okay," says Sean, my communications director. "It was your first televised one. You'll get better."

Fucking Sean.

"Seriously?" I look to Bruce.

"Well," he says with a shrug, "you missed the first question, and they were lobbing you easy pitches."

Fucking Bruce. He loves baseball. And baseball metaphors.

I sneer at them. "You know I hate stools."

"Megan," Sean says calmly, "it wasn't the stools. You were supposed to highlight the areas we discussed—housing, transportation, educa-tion. I know you think you did well, because the audience laughed, but the papers aren't going to report that. This is serious. They want to write about your positions."

I feel (and probably look) severely wounded.

"Look, shake it off," Sean instructs. "It'll get better."

I go home and pour myself an enormous glass of wine. One debate down, seventy-four to go.

• • •

Sean and Bruce turn out to not be entirely full of shit. It does get better. We hire a bunch of brilliant spin doctors from Chicago whom I fondly refer to as "the Machine." Under the Machine's tutelage, I learn the balance between being someone you want to go honky-tonking with and someone you want to have run your city. I learn how to dress and how to speak. I learn how to sit on a stool. But I'm not entirely full of shit either. It matters that I treat people like people, instead of votes.

By late May, my campaign signs sprout up on the city's lawns like wild onions, first on the east side of town, where the hipsters and pour-over coffee drinkers live, then on the north side, where you find primarily Black neighborhoods, most of which are critically under-funded. The wildly diverse south side joins in by June, and finally, the more affluent west side. Suddenly, I have donors. I have volunteers. I have press. I don't get big business or big Jesus (which here, is big business); I get the fire department, small business, and John Prine. And of course, I have Bruce and Max. After twenty years of living together, of growing numb to each other's charm, even they're drinking the Megan Barry Kool-Aid.

· · ·

Elections are never clean—despite promises on both sides to keep it to policy, to never be personal, to keep petty attacks to a minimum. We all do okay on this front. Until the runoff. In the August 6 general election, no one gets more than 50 percent of the vote—the magic number. I'm in the political chute and civility goes out the window. It's me and Opponent B.

They come for Bruce first. And thankfully, he's downright jovial when the shit slinging begins. Along with being a tenured business professor at Vanderbilt, Bruce has been a columnist for various alt-weeklies in Nashville since the 1990s. He lives to write about a hotheaded politician fumbling the ball. Opponent B finds an old piece where Bruce calls out "the Jesus Industrial Complex" and takes out radio ads claiming that Bruce is a godless Jew from New York who, if I'm elected, will plummet Nashville into an atheist hellscape. Opponent B is then quoted saying that everywhere he goes, voters are worried about electing a *woman* whose husband will really be in charge *and* (this is his coup) that said husband, Bruce Barry, is a card-carrying member of the ACLU. Bruce is practically glowing.

Then they come for Max, which is different. Max has nothing to do with any of this. He's just a kid, and a good one, maximally gentle and kind. What makes it worse is that Max knows Opponent B's family. He went to the same school as Opponent B's kids and worked summers at the local swim club where he made Opponent B's kids PB&J and hotdogs for lunch. He knows the family and they know him. Nonetheless, the whisper campaign whispers on undeterred.

Max is a bad seed.

Max gets high.

Max is out of control.

I remind the press that Max is away in Washington State at college and Max is not running for office. This is the only time I want to be ugly, but I don't, even though all I would need to dig for dirt on my opponent would be a plastic spork. We do our best to be decent. And mostly, we are. It pays off. We get the support of two candidates who didn't make the runoff and their volunteers. Hopefully, on September 10 we'll get their votes.

• • •

"There's nothing else left to do, Meggie, except rise and shine and greet the day. Oh, and go vote!" Bruce hands me coffee as I'm getting dressed. It's Election Day. He's been up for hours, patiently waiting for me to stir, which happens around 6:45 AM. Our voting routine for as long as I can remember has always been to walk to our polling location and do it together. When Max was little, he would come along too. He liked to push the buttons. During the 2000 presidential election, he pressed the Gore button for me and announced to the entire elementary school gym, "Dad's going to be mad, Mom. He's voting for Nader."

Bruce and I haven't always agreed on candidates and policy, but today we do.

The Curb Center at Belmont is crowded and humid. I say hello to the staff and check in, twinkling up a final time. I see my neighbors:

the guy who walks his dogs past the house every day around four, the waitress at the breakfast place up the road, the Vanderbilt kids in the rented duplex across the street. They wave to me and try to mouth "You're going to win" from across the room. They end up whispering kind of loudly and making me laugh. Our campaign slogan is "We Make Nashville." In this moment, it feels truer than ever.

I head past a pocket of women gossiping with only their eyes, step into my little booth, and inhale a brick of hot, heavy late-summer air; it's half deep breath, half prayer. I press the Megan Barry button. "If you don't believe in yourself, nobody else will believe in you either," I hear my mom say. I don't know if I believe in myself, but I believe in Nashville.

Turns out, they believe in me too.

Red Plastic Penguins

"You're the First Lady!"

The hotel lobby barista can't be older than twenty. His eyes are swimming-pool blue and gigantic, filled with enough caffeine to raise the dead and then chase away their hangovers.

I don't know what to say back to him, so I offer a stiff handshake of a grin, thinking, as the Lavazzas hiss at each other and a cone of water opens fire on the steel belly of the sink, that it's enough of a courtesy.

It isn't.

The espresso-glazed kid smiles expectantly at me.

I've been the mayor of Nashville for less than seventy-two hours, and people are getting it wrong already.

"Actually, I'm not the First Lady," I reply.

"You're *not*?" he asks, incredulous. A tiny skull on the end of a short silver chain swings from his earlobe. Nobody has ever looked more like a boutique hotel barista.

"But isn't that what they call the wife of the mayor?" he wonders, grabbing a carton of skim milk and a carton of almond. He gives me a good scan, but my ponytail and yoga pants tell no secrets. Nobody has ever looked less like the mayor.

"Well, you're *half* right," I explain. "The new mayor of Nashville is staying with you, but it's not my husband—it's me. I'm the mayor." I smile.

The words bring the frenetic choreography of coffee making to a complete stop. I watch it sink in and he nods slowly.

"Oh!" he says with a grin. "Cool!"

If he feels awkward about committing a glaring social faux pas, there's no evidence of it. He switches gears right away.

"Almond or regular?"

"Almond is great. Thanks."

The kid finishes my latte and pours Bruce a coffee from the carafe.

"Good luck with everything!" he says, sliding the molten-hot drinks across the counter in a cardboard carrier. I was hoping for "Congratulations!" but a little luck never hurt anyone. Especially not me.

• • •

Morning coffee is normally Bruce's territory, but today I'm glad to handle it. He's spent the past two years helping me run for office, so bringing him a decent cup of coffee is the least I can do. The past three days have been a blur. Both of us feel like we just stepped off a crabber from the Alaskan deep-sea-fishing show, all tender and wobbly, a little green too. In typical form, Bruce had the foresight to book us a getaway to a quirky hotel in Kentucky to get our land legs back. We arrived last night to a bottle of champagne in our room and a note of congratulations from the mayor of Louisville, but we were too tired to do anything other than collapse into the hotel sheets and sleep. We've hardly said a word to each other since we got here. It'll be a few years before we can go away like this again.

The elevator dings and the doors fold into each other, exposing a barren hallway decorated by a single red recycled-plastic penguin, roughly the size of a kindergartner. The penguins are migratory and are placed all over the building to remind you that you're sleeping in a contemporary gallery. It would be hard to forget, though, as there's a gold replica of Michelangelo's *David* by Özkaya the size of a split-level out front.

Hands full, I bang on the door with my head.

"It's open," Bruce calls.

Not helpful.

I stack the cups on top of each other and step inside. Bruce is already up, dressed, and *New York Times*—ed. He's the morning person. I'm the night bird, a balance that's worked well for us over the years. He got up early, made breakfast, and took Max to school. I handled the after-school shift—pickup, homework, dinner. We both clocked in for bedtime. One child, two parents was the right ratio. Divide and conquer was the right approach. There was enough time together and enough time away. Even though Max is in Tacoma studying communications and likely experimenting with legal weed, Bruce and I haven't really changed our routine. It ain't broke.

"You're dressed already!" I almost-gasp. I don't know why I sound surprised. I'm not. "I was hoping we could hop back in bed. Don't you want to laze around? We can watch some bad TV, have sex, order room service . . ."

These are the only things I want to do for the next few days.

Bruce makes a face at the mention of sex. I can see him itching in his skin. He's never been the hot-blooded type, but our house has been "headquarters" for the past seven hundred days, a certified "no intimacy" zone.

I set down the coffees and wrap my arms around his waist, pulling him toward the bed. His body stiffens and he twists away from me.

"I'm already up, Meggie. I'm going to read the paper. Let me do a little work this morning. Maybe later."

But probably not. After two years of proofreading my speeches, zipping up my dresses, and living in Megan Barry Mission Control, I'm sure the thing Bruce needs a vacation from most is me.

I lie back into the slow-sinking hotel pillow and take in a direct view of the David's perfectly symmetrical butt cheeks out the window. At this point, I have a better chance with him than my husband. I close my eyes, remembering what the woman at check-in said.

"Our red penguins move all around the hotel. You can even take one to dinner if you like."

I'm hoping it doesn't come to that.

• • •

After a couple of days of bourbon and seventeen episodes of *Law & Order*, we head back to Nashville to prepare for my inauguration. Technically it's fall, but temperatures are in the nineties. The leaves are melting off the trees and turning to glue on the sidewalk, battered by furious bouts of afternoon rain. It's a Wednesday, but I'm not sure that Wednesdays matter in my new line of work.

Max is coming tonight. He's flying in from Washington around 3 PM, and I'm guessing he won't have packed anything remotely suitable to wear. He's over six feet tall and increasingly shaggy. Shining him up takes a little more artistry than hitting Supercuts and grabbing some slacks at Target. He doesn't need to be a Jonas brother, but I'd love for him to not look like a roadie tonight. I consider asking Bruce to run to the mall, but I get the sense that he's done being my errand boy.

I begin a text message, trying to put a little spin on the ball, like the Machine taught me:

> Hi! Good news! Charles is able to squeeze you in for a haircut this afternoon. Just a trim. Nothing crazy.

I decide not to tell him about the three outfit options I left on his bed. Max is Max. He shows up as himself wherever he goes. I love this about him, but I also love public trust, and public trust is important. I won, but it's not like it was a landslide.

I wait for him to respond. Fifteen minutes go by.

Nothing.

I wait ten more.

Nothing.

I try again.

> Hi! Sorry. Just checking in to make sure you got my last message. Love you!

Normally, at this point the overbearing mother would go ahead and make the call to her son. The son would pick up, probably roll his eyes, and begrudgingly agree to entertain his mother's ridiculous request to shower and shave. But that's not our dynamic. Max wouldn't pick up. We're texters. Bruce is Max's phone person. And there's no way that Bruce Barry is going to tell his long-haired son to get some sort of "summer in Nantucket" makeover.

My inauguration is on Friday and my team has been busy planning for the event. They've been given access to the old mayor's office, a stodgy and terrible first-floor office at the Metro Courthouse. The design story is "imposing" and "masculine," Stalinist but with a Southern twist. The walls are painted something Benjamin Moore might call "Bus Station Yellow," while the carpet is more "Regional Airport Brown."

By the time I walk in, everyone else is on their third cup of coffee.

"Are you ready for Friday?" Claudia asks. She smiles at me, lifting a curtain of blonde hair from her shoulder. Claudia ran my campaign and has stepped gracefully into the role of senior adviser, which is good because I need her advice. She's brilliant and wildly organized. I watched her transform Team Megan Barry from a pirate ship to an ant colony. Before helping us morph into a political superorganism, she was a senior aide for Al Gore, so she comes with experience (more than I have). From the beginning, she has seemed completely undaunted by the prospect of helping run one of America's fastest-growing cities. I, however, am daunted.

"Ready or not, here I come," I respond with a shrug.

"Everything is going to be great," she assures me. I don't even know what everything she's talking about.

Across the mustard-colored expanse, Sean is on his phone, pacing. He mercifully agreed to stay on as communications director and manage press for me, a big task considering that I'm a blue woman in a red state. I think he loves his job, but I'll never understand why. Our hands are full, but we exchange chin tilts and I continue toward what will soon be my office, which faces Public Square, home to occasional concerts, spontaneous soccer games, and frequent pigeon-on-pigeon warfare.

Tall, handsome Patrick, my scheduler (and my fashion inspiration), sings out, "Are you ready for your big day on Friday?" He hands me a copy of the upcoming day's events. The list includes a prayer breakfast, a trip to Andrew Jackson's Hermitage for a swearing-in ceremony for new American citizens, and then the inauguration.

"And just so you know," he adds, making a sad face, "they're calling for rain."

My eyes travel over the agenda, which is color coded in a way I don't yet understand.

"Oh well! Maybe it's good luck?" I speculate.

"I like that," he says with a smile, revealing two rows of teeth that should be in a Royal Doulton museum. I make a mental note to ask him later who his dentist is.

Elease is in the old mayor's office, trying to find a surface on which to set a vase of star-shaped lilies. A shower of vibrant orange pollen falls onto the carpet.

"Sorry," she says, wincing. "These came for you. No card."

"It's fine, Elease. Thank you."

Elease, my assistant, is the kind of person universally described as wonderful. She is warm and hardworking, and her idealism will hold me accountable. She worked in the Metro Council office for years when I was a councilperson, and I trust her with everything. I'm probably far more nervous about letting her down than she is about disappointing me. And rightly so.

"Let me know if you need anything," she tells me before leaving and returning to her desk. What I need is a Bloody Mary, but I keep that to myself.

Elease comes in to give me a coffee and to remind me that even though I'm not officially the mayor yet, I've got folks who already want to meet with me in the conference room and they are waiting. They are the Tennessee Department of Transportation (or "T-Dot," a sassy little nickname they've given themselves).

I look over at the flowers, rubbing a petal as I head to my meeting, and wonder if people send flowers when a man wins the election.

Just as the meeting with the T-Dot guys begins, I glance at my phone as Max texts me back.

Mom, I'm not cutting my hair.

• • •

The inauguration ceremony is beautiful, even though it pisses down rain and we're tasked with creating an atmosphere of hope and freedom in the ballroom of a convention center that also happens to host the Tennessee GOP banquet. The Stratford High School marching band plays a fight song, and Jason Isbell and Amanda Shires, Americana icons, sing a ballad about the South, the kind of rich, lilting, folkloric music that makes people from simple places suddenly proud and heartsick for their hometowns. There are Kurdish and mariachi dance groups and a reading from our youth poet laureate, which truthfully, I didn't know we had until I saw the program. There is an atmosphere of hope, freedom, and progress. The room is buzzing.

Max shows up with his hair pulled back in a ponytail and looks presentable. Thank goodness.

Bruce smiles at me, obviously proud. I'm still reveling in his ridiculous belief in me that turned out not to be so ridiculous after all. I smile back.

When I step onto the stage, the audience is roaring low and constant like an ocean. I'm not humble, but I'm smart enough to know the noise is for us, not me. The city represented in this room is no antique—it's progressive, dynamic, diverse, and *going places*. This is as much Nashville's inauguration as mine; it's her coming-out, the heartbeat of our city singing and dancing and rejoicing. I'm an accessory to this moment, not the center of it, and I can't help but feel like a part of my victory was being different when Nashville was ready for something different than what had come before. I look out not into an audience but into a movement, a community, and fall in love with every face, every voice. Two of my primary opponents, Howard Gentry and Charles Robert Bone, are with their daughters, Taylor and Margaret. I see my brother-in-law and my niece, Lilly. I want to make these little girls proud. I want them to think that having a woman mayor isn't unusual or novel and they can just focus on the kind of mayor I will be and the legacy I will leave.

I'm reminded again that our campaign slogan doesn't stop with the campaign. "We Make Nashville" isn't just a snappy saying. It's the belief that will carry us forward; it's the promise I can make to my community.

I'm going to do this. And I'm going to do it right.

"While we are different as individuals, together, we make Nashville," I read into the mic. "We make Nashville a vibrant, exciting city that is the envy of a nation. We make Nashville—each and every one of you in this room."

This is the electricity. This is why I'm here. Nashville is still glowing. The adrenaline of the campaign hasn't aged a day. What felt like the end of a long race is the beginning of something bigger, more challenging, more promising, and more consuming. Whatever that something is, I pledge my loyalty to it.

Hope, fear, and shapewear carry me through the next several days. Diet Coke too. I go home to sleep, take my shoes off, and say goodbye to Max. Reluctantly, he agrees that he'll come back and take part in the odd thing here or there. Bruce has gone back to his usual routine: teaching, watching the Mets, sipping whiskey on the porch, and reading the *Atlantic*. Everybody who was worried about Bruce and his ACLU card being in charge and running the show can take a load off.

Nothing about my life is the same. I'm the one who has solemnly sworn to govern the city and I feel totally alone. I'm wishing I had one of those red penguins for company about now.

Solvable Problems

I sink down into the nubby gray fabric of my new couch, running my hand over the tweed cushions, sucking in the smell of Scotchgard and West Elm until a slight headache begins to form at my temples. It's Sunday and the Metro Courthouse is a ghost town. I'm just here to finish decorating our space, which I'm proud to say looks much less like a humidor than it did when we came into office.

In a blistering six-week reno, we painted over the jaundiced walls in a lovely bridal white and ripped up the carpet to reveal concrete floors. We had them refinished and buffed until they were shiny and slick enough for Scott Hamilton to hit his triple salchow. The room feels light and airy, like a few well-placed orchids could actually stand a chance. With the help of a designer, we've created "zones." There's a loosely defined "reading zone" with a low-slung bookshelf, a "meeting zone" with more nubby modern furniture, and most critically, a "coffee zone," loaded up with local beans and a grinder. We'll see how long we can hold out before swallowing our pride and switching to K-Cups.

"The zones encourage intimacy," the designer assured us. "They help people engage meaningfully with each other."

We ran a campaign from my dining room table with my dirty laundry and bad dogs in plain sight. We're past the point of needing zones, but it does look good, and everybody on staff seems into the Apple Store aesthetic. My credit card would have preferred a less dramatic transformation. Even at the mayoral level, a public service salary is a public service salary. You're not going to get very far at Crate & Barrel.

To be sure we don't forget where we came from, I traded out the piano-sized oak desk in my office for a gray, mottled wooden dining table flanked by two rounded, high-back gold-flaked chairs. Collaboration, conversation, and coming together worked for us. Transparency worked for us. They're still working. A few months in and my approval rating is through the roof. Nashville and I are in our honeymoon phase.

My most enthusiastic critics have lost interest and turned their attention to the 2016 Republican primary, which as far as I can tell is one protracted episode of *Dukes of Hazzard*. Ben Carson makes sure everyone knows he's a neurosurgeon. Ted Cruz makes sure everyone knows he's a Christian. Rand Paul makes sure everyone knows he's a different kind of Republican. Donald J. Trump calls everyone stupid and ugly. Poor Megyn Kelly wishes Fox had hired Dog the Bounty Hunter to moderate. It's right-wing bedlam and Bruce Barry is in heaven taking it all in. At the request of my team, he agreed to stop writing inflammatory articles for his beloved alt-weeklies. His flavor is lemon sour, writing that always grazes satire if it doesn't grab onto it entirely. The kind of undiplomatic stuff we love. Or loved. He doesn't seem to mind much about stepping back, which is a bit of a relief. But stepping back seems to be his MO these days. I'm not sure he fully believes I'm the mayor.

Bruce is invited to everything but comes to nothing. He isn't interested in missing work to hold my handbag at a ribbon cutting, and though he was very clear that there would be no playing "First Gentleman" for him, I struggled to believe it. He wore a button, for Christ's sake. He wanted this too. If I had more time to worry, it would be a troubling turnaround, but I don't have time. We hit the ground running, just like we promised.

The team and I have entered a blissful season of yeses. We're getting shit done.

Do we want to upgrade traffic signals? Yes!

Should there be more diversity in metro government? Yes!

Can we work toward more affordable housing? Yes!

I appoint a chief diversity officer to make sure our administration reflects the people we serve, which, increasingly, are all people—all races, faiths, genders, and sexual orientations. We spend a lot of time working with the Office of New Americans, welcoming our newest community members and equipping them with the resources they need to feel safe and settled. With every positive step forward, we brace ourselves for blowback from a conservative army of swinging dicks and talking heads, but the crowd who insisted for two years that I was nothing but a tube of lipstick with my husband's politics has dissolved. Nobody says anything.

The next project and the most ambitious item on our agenda is transportation. We're quietly putting together a large-scale plan to reduce congestion in our growing city, which is basically three interstates tied in a series of complex sailor's knots choking the downtown core. The crown jewel of said plan will be a light rail system. Accessible, affordable transportation is the hallmark of a modern city. At least, *I* think so.

Suddenly, I hear a voice from outside say, "Hello?"

My new couch sits under a pair of large windows so that when I need air (which is often) I can stand up, crank open the first-floor casement, unfurl the leaded-glass panes, and breathe it in. There's a large marble ledge right outside with a wide perch. Sometimes, I hoist myself up, crawl out, and sit, so I can look out over Public Square. It drives my staff crazy. They say, "You might fall," "Someone might grab you and pull you out," or (my favorite, from Sean) "It doesn't look very mayoral."

I pull my body up and look down, squinting against the sun. A young man in a nice suit waves up at me.

"Howdy," I say.

"I am vondering if you help me?" he asks in a very Russian accent. Bruce has put me through enough Tarkovsky; I could pick it out anywhere. "I find the mayor's office for meeting my boss has with mayor on Monday. I what you call scout, see?"

"Congratulations! You found me!" I shout down to him, moving farther out onto the ledge. "You're at the right place. Who's your boss?"

"Russian ambassador, Sergey Kislyak. He has meeting with mayor. Thank you for help," he says.

"Sure! Tell your boss I look forward to meeting him on Monday," I say with a smile.

The scout stops and looks up at me more closely. "You, the mayor?"

To be fair, I'm dressed like I'm on my way to a youth soccer tournament and—the elephant on the ledge—I am a woman.

"Yep."

He laughs, shakes his head, and walks away.

He doesn't believe I'm the mayor either, but I'm starting to. I head back to my dining table / desk and begin rearranging.

. . .

On the first true morning of fall, there's belligerent fog outside suspended between the pavement and the streetlamps, making it look darker outside than it should be. I come clipping down the stairs in my black boots.

"You're wearing *that* dress to work?" Bruce asks, raising his eyebrows. I've got on a black, long-sleeve, A-line dress with a leather piece around the waist. I think it makes me look slimmer.

"I like it. What's wrong with it?" I ask him back.

Bruce's fashion sense isn't something I've cared about for years, but the fact that he's noticed is something.

"It just looks kind of *funereal*, that's all," he says with a shrug.

Bruce loves a word like *funereal*, but it's not the exact descriptor I was going for.

If we were still campaigning or living in the world before it, we would sit down together and debate whether *funereal* should be a word at all. We would go through the headlines. Bruce would wonder what the hell happened to real journalism, and I would tell him not to be so cynical (though in the cynicism department, I'm a close second). But this world is different. We've had twenty years of mornings together, but suddenly there's a barrenness and business to them. I stepped into my new life and Bruce stepped back into his old one. We make a great team. We bring out the best in each other. We're funny and affable. People like us. Good luck finding a better premise for a rom-com than "the ethics professor and the politician." But without a crowd, a campaign, or a kid kicking around, we don't really know how to be with each other.

A white Tahoe is idling along the curb on the side of our house. Through the kitchen window, I see smoke from the tailpipe curling up in the new chill of the early-morning air. I'm relieved to see it. Everyone needs a getaway car.

"It looks like my ride's here," I say.

"You have to go already? Don't you want any coffee?" he asks.

Marital discord or not, coffee is the most sacred of our rites.

I look over at him and frown. He's also dressed for work in a black T-shirt, black jeans, and a ratty sports coat. It must be a teaching day.

If it weren't, he would be wearing a black T-shirt, black jeans, and an equally tattered zipper sweatshirt.

"I don't think I have time. The car is already here. I must have missed something in my schedule. When these guys show up, I'm supposed to be ready."

One of the major perks of my job is not having to drive anymore, not anywhere. The police chief has assigned a rigorous security detail, a rotating cast of officers who stay with me most of the time.

I reach for a travel mug, pour in some dark roast, and add milk, a dash of cinnamon, and Truvia. Bruce makes a face. He's fundamentally opposed to things in coffee. Especially Truvia.

"I need to figure out how not to be so rushed in the morning. I'm taking suggestions," I say with a frazzled breath.

"Why don't you just get up earlier?" he asks, smiling. "Then we can have coffee together."

Of course, he's spot-on as a morning person and, I'm glad to see, willing to dispense advice that might be helpful.

I look out the window and, impossibly, the Tahoe is smokier and more impatient.

I wait for a moment. I'm not sure for what.

"I better go." I sigh. "See you later? I have a dinner if you want to come. I can get Patrick to send you the details."

"Not tonight, but thanks," Bruce says with a grimace.

He would rather do anything than sit at a numbered table eating chicken and watching me hit my talking points. I can't decide if it hurts or not. I take another stab at the conversation, still not ready to leave.

"You know, yesterday they told me the Tahoe is a police car. It has lights and everything."

Bruce looks up from reading the newspaper. "Is this information I need to know?"

"Nope." I smile.

I walk over, give Bruce a kiss on the cheek, gather up my briefcase, and head to the door.

"What time do you think you'll be done with the dinner thing? Any idea?" he asks.

"Nope." I smile again. "The days are really long right now. I'm sure it'll get better."

But it doesn't. Connecting with 681,000 Nashvillians takes all the time, energy, and love I can muster, and most nights I don't take my heels off and limp up onto our porch until about 10 PM. Bruce doesn't wait up for me and I don't wake up early for him.

● ● ●

Bruce's phone rings on a Saturday in November. It's Max. He's about halfway through his degree at the University of Puget Sound (fondly referred to as UPS by everybody except the United Parcel Service), but I'm pretty sure the career track he's chosen is something like "after-party DJ," although I like to think of it as communications. Not the ideal trajectory for the mayor's kid.

When Max was growing up, I worked a lot and traveled a lot. Bruce was the parent at home, the one to pack the school lunches and coach baseball. He helped with the homework and painstakingly washed Max's hair with Rid shampoo, combing out every little bit of lice and reminding him not to borrow his friend's sketchy hat again. He was in the emergency room when Max broke his wrist. He was the adventurer who drove Max across Kansas every summer to camp in Colorado. I was busy those years. I'm still busy. And it shows.

"Hey, Max!" Bruce greets him with a hell of a lot more warmth than I've felt from him over the past few months. I'm horrified by the flash of jealousy.

Max's voice swells through the receiver on the other side of the room. I soften when the sound hits my ears. Max is a giant in all ways. Big guy, big laugh, big love. He has no idea where he's going in life, but for some reason, absolutely everybody he meets wants to go with him. He is also anxious, and always has been underneath the teddy bear suit and the aura of "chill" he projects to the world. During the campaign, he had helped me find the humor. Together we watched Opponent B's online ads for mayor, slickly designed by a big-time ad firm to mimic Matthew McConaughey's ads for some car. Instead of Matthew, Opponent B was behind the wheel endlessly driving around Nashville, looking and looking.

"Doesn't he know that Ashley Madison is available on his phone now? He can stop driving around," Max had quipped.

During the race there were a lot of rumors about Max, most of which I was sure were bullshit. Max is doing drugs. Max is failing out of school. Max is a pothead (we were all pretty sure that one was true). Lately, I'm not sure what's true and what's not. He's been hard to get ahold of, and when I have talked to him, he has sounded disconnected. On more than one occasion it's hurled me into a state of spiraling worries, and I've wondered aloud to Bruce, "Do you think we need to talk to him?"

"He's just a kid," Bruce always says. "He's figuring it all out. Go easy on him."

He's usually right about these things.

Bruce is laughing, pacing the length of the kitchen island, and talking about Hank the dog's latest attempt at squirrel-napping. Five minutes later, they hang up.

"How did he sound?" I ask, my words a flimsy disguise for what I really want to know:

Did he sound high?

Is he going to class?

Has he lost any weight?

Are his grades still shit?

"He's fine." Bruce smiles but not at me. Our dogs, Hank and Boris, stare up at Bruce with longing and neuroses in their beady eyes, tails wagging clumsily into each other, with no spatial awareness whatsoever.

"You want to go for a walk?" He smiles at them, mussing the hair on their smelly heads. They lick their chops and stifle a string of whimpers. I wonder how it is that two rescue dogs with four brain cells between them can figure out how to get through to Bruce and I can't.

"See you in a bit, Meggie," he says, leaving the house in an ecstatic tangle of leashes and canines.

Why didn't I just go with him?

I pull out my chair at the dining table and check my email, diving into the comfort of solvable problems like traffic lights and bike lanes.

Details

Late November 2015 lies across Nashville like a wet rag on feverish skin. The daily highs have been in the sixties, but dusk is blowing in earlier and earlier on the kind of balmy wind that makes you check the batteries in your flashlights and stalk the local storm watcher on Twitter. Daily stabs of lightning threaten to loosen summer's grip, but none of us know if a storm is actually coming. Tennessee is capable of producing all four seasons but careful not to promise them.

My eyes open to a milky-dark morning out the window with neither moon nor sun. Just a few inconsequential stars belonging to no constellations perforate the denseness of the sky. The reality of the day settles in.

It's a Wednesday.

I'm in bed.

I'm the mayor.

I have a budget meeting, a lunch meeting, and then a pile of proposals to read through.

Transportation.

The transportation plan is happening. *Really* happening. And even to my opponents, mostly the kind of puffy white guys you expect, the urgency to do *something* is clear. Big tech is coming. Developers are here. Gentrification is real. We're congested and frustrated and unprepared for what we're becoming: an *it* city.

The benefits of this explosive growth are obvious. We inherited a mountain of debt from the previous administration, who probably inherited debt from the folks before them. The city needs money. Badly. But we can't go selling our soul. The bigger Nashville gets and the faster it gets there, the more expensive and less inclusive it becomes. Low-income residents get pushed out to make room for South-curious Brooklynites. The people who helped build our thriving economy lose access to it. We need to make sure everyone can get to work, and even though it won't be cheap, a light rail system will do that.

Plus, as Bruce consistently reminded me when I was campaigning, it wouldn't exactly hurt global boiling if there were fewer F-150s clogging up the interstate.

I turn over to his side of the bed and stare into the man-shaped grooves in the linen just as sunlight begins to drip in. It's 6:30 AM. He's already up and probably half a pot of coffee deep. I haul my ass out from under the covers. The only times Bruce and I have together now are the mornings.

When I finally clack down the stairs in my heels, the kitchen smells like whole wheat toast and muddy paws. Bruce is sitting behind a wall of newspaper.

"Morning," he announces, lazily cheerful.

"Morning," I say back. "Guess what? I'm looking at proposals for the light rail today."

"Oh good," he says with a grin. "Dogs have been out."

I can tell the dogs have been out; their legs are soaking wet and straggly and they look thrilled with themselves. It's the "oh good" that confounds me. Three months ago, the mere mention of a light rail system would send Bruce into a state of ecstasy I've been incapable of inspiring since Y2K.

He taps a strip of petrified crust on the side of his plate, and I just watch him for a moment as he considers which *New York Times* op-ed to praise or grumble about. He's mostly given up reading anything local. Too much me, I guess.

Are you okay? Are we okay? I want to ask but don't. The idea of us not being okay is almost silly. I tell myself it will blow over, which is the kind of thing politicians like to say, even to themselves. I tell myself, *We've been married twenty years*, which is the kind of thing people who have been married for twenty years tell themselves when they know something is very wrong.

By the time I can shake my head passive-aggressively at him and fill my travel mug, the Tahoe is already outside waiting. I grab a pile of books and hook my briefcase through my little finger.

"I'm letting the pups out again. I'll make sure the side gate is closed," I murmur.

"Sounds good." Bruce appears to nod from behind the Arts section. He doesn't ask when I'll be home. He doesn't look at me.

• • •

The morning's attempt at frost nearly sends me backwards onto my ass when I step outside. I'm carrying too much shit, like always.

Sergeant Forrest, my detail, is immediately out of the car and coming around to help me.

"Good morning, ma'am!" he says with a grin. "Can I take some of that stuff for you? You look great, by the way. I love the dress!"

"Thanks!" I say, handing him a couple of books, hardbacks about the city for the office waiting area.

Sergeant Rob Forrest is handsome—Sterling Cooper Draper Pryce handsome—but with a loaded gun and a Southern accent. He's head of my security and today he's dressed in a gray suit and pink tie, a nice combination with his thinning silver hair and blue eyes. There isn't a fleck of lint on him, and he strikes me as the kind of guy who pays attention to the details. I'm the third mayor he's worked with. Of the officers on my team, he's the closest to me in age. Because we're of a generation that can hold a conversation without taking a break to check Instagram, we're getting along well. I'm trying to keep things casual with all the security guys, sitting up front and telling self-deprecating jokes, hoping that when they're off, they say things like "Megan is the best mayor we've ever worked with!" and "I'm so glad she's our mayor!"

Sergeant Forrest opens the side gate and then the passenger-side door, a startling act of chivalry. Bruce is from New York, where when it comes to holding doors, pulling out chairs, and giving up seats on the subway, it's every man, woman, or child for themselves.

I shuffle to the curb in my heels and pull myself into the Tahoe, trying not to break the zipper of my clingy houndstooth number in the process.

A rush climbs from my sternum to my cheeks.

Sergeant Forrest is watching me.

I meet his eye for half a second.

Something shifts.

As far as cheap thrills go, being looked at by a man is one they keep up by the register, but it's been a long time. I'll take it. Thankfully, he shuts the door quickly behind me.

"Mayor on the move," he says into a whoosh of radio static. Then he smiles again.

"Ma'am, that really is a great dress."

We drive away from the house, and I don't look back.

I spend the day thinking about fixing potholes, repaving sidewalks, and that possible split second of lust. I spend the next two weeks beginning formal plans for the light rail system and sitting in traffic with Sergeant Forrest. It's a silly, innocent crush. I tell myself again, it will blow over.

• • •

The second people start chucking their jack-o'-lanterns and Costco brings out the industrial-sized spools of ribbon, it's Christmas. Or it might as well be. Public Square is filled with large velvet bows and wreaths the size of kiddie pools. Old candy canes made of frizzy tinsel hang tight from the lampposts, which looks cheap and garish all day and fabulous and magical after 6 PM when the lights flick on. One afternoon, a forty-two-foot Norway spruce arrives outside my office window, which like all windows in city hall is bordered in red, green, and blue lights for the holiday, a selection of colors I'm told is festive but not demonstratively Christian. Elease orders the eggnog-flavored K-Cups and keeps a poinsettia on her desk. Patrick starts dressing like Bing Crosby. I surrender myself to the fact that nobody is going to get any meaningful work done until January. It's hot cocoa and singing until 2016. I congratulate myself for two successful months of leadership and let the yuletide glee take over. Bruce is suddenly gleeful too and less averse to accompanying me to events. He's always had a remarkable amount of Christmas spirit for a Jew.

After a week of slow dressing in melon-sized baubles and snowflakes, in the first week of December, the giant Public Square tree is ready for her moment. The tree lighting was one of the few important family photo ops I'd hoped Max would attend, but he left just after Thanksgiving not wildly pleased with me. I spoke to him over the break about coming back more often. I told him I missed him, which is true.

Also true is that press-wise, he's a bit of a shadowy figure and it would be much better for my future in politics if he could be less shadowy. I had said it as diplomatically as possible and sold it as hard as I could.

"Of course, I will pay for the flights!"

"You can think of it like a vacation!"

"You can spend time with your friends!"

He quickly reminded me that wearing khakis at a church breakfast and getting his picture taken so that people keep liking me is not vacation.

He spent most of his time at home lying in bed with Hank listening to De La Soul and vaping, which I don't know much about but can't be good for him or the dog. Predictably, Bruce was the one to drop him off at the airport. I didn't get a chance to say goodbye, or I didn't make a point of it.

"I think he's pissed off about the hair thing," I tell Bruce on the way to Public Square, turning my head toward him. We're in the Tahoe together, but he's in the back. It had never occurred to me to slide in next to him. Sergeant Forrest is driving.

I've been looking forward to the annual tree lighting ceremony. Some sweet kids from the Edgehill Bike Club are going to join me to help flip the switch. There'll be free cider and a good choir (there are no bad choirs in Nashville). Gnash, the Nashville Predators mascot, will be there to rope me into some kind of improv pantomime performance for which I'll be entirely unprepared but will participate in enthusiastically. Dancing with a seven-foot-tall saber-tooth tiger is great for the approval rating. Not that mine needs help.

I go over my last conversation with Max in my head as we drive slowly through the city. I had asked him to cut his hair to appear more professional. Then I demanded that he cut his hair because he was starting to look like "a fucking roadie." The truth is I don't even mind the hair, as long as he can keep it more Kenny G than Slash. And I like roadies. I'm sure I got the roadie vote.

"Does he hate me?" I venture, sounding pitiful and teenaged.

Bruce's jaw tightens, which normally means he's about to say something he knows I won't like.

"Meggie, he just doesn't want to be a part of the whole mayor thing."

He cracks his window and stares at some kids walking arthritically in stiff new cowboy boots down Broadway. He and Max were both pretty into the whole mayor thing when I was running.

"What do you mean?" I prod.

Bruce shakes his head and says, "I mean it's your job, not his. You're on his ass all the time. Who cares if he watches you carve a turkey?"

"Aren't you worried?" I ask. Based on my estimations, which have been honed by years of on again, off again Weight Watchers and a steady stream of Jenny Craig commercials (when Queen Latifah was the spokeswoman), Max is very suddenly about forty pounds overweight. He spends all his time sleeping and playing video games. He doesn't have any direction. He doesn't appear to care about anything.

"He's having a hard time," Bruce says, nodding. "We need to be there for him, not shove him on a stage and tell him to smile."

It's a low blow. Bruce is excellent at making me sound like a monster and he knows it.

I don't say anything back. I just pull down the passenger-side mirror to reapply my lipstick. I wanted to go with red initially, but something about wearing "fuck me" lipstick (which is basically the same as Christmas lipstick) in the same car as the man I'm married to and the man that I look forward to driving to work with felt confusing and morally ambiguous. I went with the cranberry instead. Even though nobody's fucking me.

When the Tahoe pulls into the garage, my team is waiting.

"I'm sorry," Bruce says, jaw still clenching and releasing, clenching, and releasing.

"It's fine," I spit back at him. But it isn't.

Bruce opens his door, gets out, and walks straight over to Sean to say hello. Claudia gives him a big hug, and Patrick, as always, looks amazing. My door opens and Sergeant Forrest is there, smiling.

• • •

I'm not sure when I start calling him Rob, whether I'm formally invited to or I just take the initiative myself after hearing his name bounce around the office enough times. Either way, we spend fourteen hours a day together, so it doesn't take long for "Sergeant Forrest" and "ma'am" to lose their luster. I prefer "Megan" anyway; it's a crucial part of the "approachable mayor" brand we've been selling for the past two years.

"Call me Megan, please," I say over and over.

He hangs onto "ma'am" until January. Barely.

Winter makes a brief showing with a series of still, sunny days when people put shoes on their dogs and keep their faucets on drip. After spending the holidays in "What a great couple!" mode, entertaining and cranking out banter, trying to believe the hype we were building, Bruce and I are more exhausted with each other than ever. He's bothered that I'm always on my phone twinkling up at someone, and I'm bothered that he won't twinkle up at all for me. We conferred briefly about our holiday party, something we've both loved every year except this one, but I didn't have a Friday open to get shit-faced while he made a test pitcher of a specialty cocktail. Family came to town. I put in an appearance at his work party, and he came to mine. On New Year's Eve, we kissed in front of the cameras on Broadway, because like his attendance, it was required.

Nobody would know we were falling apart. Max was too reclusive over Christmas to even talk to me (though he continued to dialogue with Bruce on the subjects of dogs and football). The tension is subtle, wispy, and elegant. Even I'm not sure *falling apart* is the right term. Still, *apart* feels more appropriate than anything else.

• • •

Bruce is getting ready to head out to a late-afternoon meeting. The city is covered in black ice, but being a man of principle, he is fine to take the bus.

"I'm sure we could drop you off on the way," I tell him.

Rob is about to pick me up for an event. I'm wearing a great dress. My cleavage is a little too pronounced, which Sean will want to mention but won't know how to navigate.

It's funny. Being attracted to Rob doesn't make me care about Bruce any less. I don't want him to get frostbite. I would worry if he wasn't home when he said he was going to be. I love him. I *like* him.

He pulls a knit hat over his ears and glares at the shimmering street.

"All good," he mutters. He would rather do anything than be squired around town by the mayor in a mode of transportation to which he's fundamentally opposed, but I had to ask. I watch him don his backpack and head off to the bus stop. I love and like him and I'm relieved that he's gone.

Rob rolls up seconds later. I'm waiting for him.

His eyes find mine easily in the window. It's his job to watch me, and for months he's done it expertly, standing to my left at every lectern, leading me through crowded rooms with a hand on the lowest part of my back, just watching, eyes settling on my neck when I take long sips of coffee, on my lips as I answer the phone, on my legs when I unfold my body from the truck. I'm watching him too. I dress up because someone is looking, tell stories and jokes because someone is listening.

He says things like "That was amazing."

"You're making a real difference."

"You look beautiful today."

And it's exactly what I need to hear, even if he's not the one I need to hear it from.

"Where's Bruce?" he asks, walking to the door to help me with my usual armload of things. "I guess he didn't have a chance to help you."

This is a dig and I know it.

"He's gone." I roll my eyes, feeling immediately disloyal but also struck by the truth of it. Bruce *is* gone. He has been for a while.

Rob places my bags in the backseat while I step onto the running board of the Tahoe and climb in.

I settle in my seat for the ride to the dinner. The Tahoe is still in park. We aren't moving.

"What's up?" I ask.

He turns to face me, and the spice of his cologne finds its way into my nose. Nervous (and handsome), he hesitates, drawing his lower lip into his mouth for a moment.

"It would really make my life easier," he takes a breath, "if, during the time we work together, when there's something on the schedule that might involve your friend Liz, I'm not assigned to work or cover that event. I'm sure you understand why."

He's suddenly sheepish. I don't set the security detail's schedules, as far as I know. I thought he did. I also don't know why he gives a shit about Liz, whom I drink martinis and gossip with several times a month.

"I don't understand. You'll need to be more specific," I say. Now, I'm just curious.

He goes on, "I'm sure Liz told you. We had an affair a long time ago when I worked in vice. It's over, but my wife still thinks it's going on. I don't want to fight with her if she sees Liz's name on your schedule."

"Liz has never mentioned you." I shrug, surprised, then embarrassed for him. I'm sure if you have an affair with someone, you at least want to be memorable enough that you come up occasionally when she's a few drinks in.

"Oh," he says with a frown, "my wife, Sheri, still doesn't know for certain that anything went on, but she's been focused on it for the last ten years and accuses me a lot. She still thinks Liz and I are sleeping together."

He laughs a little uneasily and lets this moment of intimacy between us hang in the air.

I don't know what to say and blurt out the first thing that comes to mind.

"You've never confessed? *All* those times she's accused you, you never told your wife you cheated. For *ten* years?" I sit back in my seat. "That sounds like a little slice of hell. For you and for her."

His laugh is loud and earnest now. His watch jangles. We're comfortable. He trusts me. It feels better than it should.

"Nope. I'm very good at keeping secrets. I will never confess," he says, sliding his glasses down onto his nose.

I file his confession away, and he puts the car in drive.

Just Kids

I should've sat in the back.

If Rob were in the front and I were in the back, I wouldn't notice the perfect, soft sloping terrain of his skin. I wouldn't catch myself looking at his long fingers wrapped around the steering wheel and imagine what it would feel like to have them tracing the length of my jaw. If I'd sat in the back, my clothes and hair wouldn't absorb his Irish Spring soap, sugary sports drinks, and warm breath, and that combination of smells wouldn't bring a drunken flush to my cheeks in the middle of a Monday staff meeting. If I'd sat in the back like all the mayors before me, I wouldn't know that his tie was Ted Baker, and he wouldn't know that I loved it. He wouldn't ask me what music I listened to when I was seventeen years old, and I wouldn't return there, to an everlasting summer of Guess jeans, bronze-colored skin, and wine coolers. If I'd sat in the back, we would be "ma'am" and Sergeant Forrest, not Megan and Rob.

Bob Seger is on the radio, and it's raining a slow, monotonous January rain. Rob turns the Tahoe down Belmont Boulevard. We've been working together for twelve hours today, but I still don't want to go home.

"You okay?" Rob asks. I love that he asks.

"Mmmm," I murmur. I expect he knows what it means, and he does. We're comfortable enough that we can speak to each other in sounds and looks and little telepathies. Every time we do, we get a bit closer.

A gust of winter air, fresh, odorless, and stinging, comes in at me through the smallest crack in the window, and I sing badly along to Bob Seger's "Turn the Page" on the satellite radio.

He smiles at me like I'm beguiling, and I slip off a shoe, leaning back into the seat like we've got hours left to go, even though we're almost home.

"Such a good song," I say with a sigh as the wipers slow. "I quoted it in my yearbook when I was a senior."

"Moody," he declares, raising his brow the way handsome people love to do, "but very cool."

He's mocking me a bit, and it's irresistible. We stop in the wet pink glow of the stop light. He looks at me and sighs. He's been doing that a lot lately, and I lap it up. It's been a long time since I've been adored to the sounds of Bob Seger and rain on a windshield. I hate the light for changing when it does.

We turn onto my street, and I greet each family and each house. Bruce and I have been here for a long time, since we were so deep in debt and in love, we didn't think we'd ever find our way out of either. We've managed to find a way out of both. I revisit the Halloween when Max wobbled down the sidewalk in a little yellow hard hat and construction vest, and we pass the spot under the hackberry tree where the Santa we used for Christmas parties would park his Corolla, far enough away from prying seven-year-old eyes. I could never decide whether the kids would be more upset that Santa didn't have a sleigh or that he *did* have a Corolla. We have so much history, but it is just that—history.

A group of tipsy undergrads hunch their shoulders and march through the drizzle toward their duplexes and triplexes and musty basement apartments. A boy who in the dark looks enough like Bruce and a girl who looks enough like me walk side by side, slightly behind the others. I can't tell if they're together, and I'm not sure why, but for a moment I'm hell-bent on knowing. They step into the sheen on the streetlight, laughing about something, and then disappear behind a plume of cigarette smoke. *They're just kids. It really doesn't matter.*

The rain falls harder again, and I want less and less to walk into the shadows of my own home, where maybe Bruce is or maybe he isn't, where maybe he'll notice me coming up the stairs, but likely, he won't.

"I don't want to go home yet." It's the most honest thing I've said in a long time. "We have to finish the song, at least this one."

Rob smiles and turns up the volume, his arm brushing against mine for long enough that it all feels like a test. We roll past the perfect white house on the corner where the Barrys live: the porch where Bruce likes to watch the Mets after work, the side gate where Hank the dog still waits faithfully at 5 PM for his kid to come home (even though he's been gone for a few years), the bare-naked boughs I've watched come to life and wither exactly twenty-two times. The bedroom light is off, and I calculate that I've spent eight thousand nights with a man who seems to love me out of habit.

I don't have to go home anymore.

We go up and down the alleyways, the dead ends, the dark places, and I sing softly along to the next song. When the puddles are still and the sky clears, Rob drops me at the gate, standing guard by the Tahoe until I'm safe inside, where nobody is waiting.

• • •

There are a hundred thousand reasons to love Bruce Barry, but as winter goes from gray to grayer, I have lost my path to all of them. The adrenaline of the election has officially cleared from our blood, and my schedule is unforgiving. Bruce is invited to everything, but he comes to nothing. He doesn't want to be my plus-one. He has a job, and he likes it. He's a brilliant and beloved professor, whom colleagues admire and trust. The people he wants to impress are enamored with him.

I am not one of those people. Not anymore.

He's heard all my stories, unfurled every mystery. I'm the side gate, the front porch, the boxwoods, just another piece of home with lipstick on.

At first, I try to wait it out. In the evenings, after Rob drops me off, I slip under the sheet and lie there thinking maybe Bruce will notice the new heat in my body or the foreign spice in his nose of someone new, of musky pine and breath mints.

Maybe it will panic him.

Maybe some kind of snarling alpha dog will awake inside him at 2 AM and he'll want to make love to me.

Maybe he'll stop me from doing what I know I'm going to do.

He lies still, peaceful, and a million miles away. I fall asleep reminding myself why I love him.

I love you because you give Boris ham.

I love you because you make me laugh.

I love you because you like to sit on the porch and just talk.

I love you because you are the smartest person I know.

I love you because you research everything.

I love you because you love Colorado.

I love you because you are my LAN administrator.

But it isn't enough.

• • •

"Keith Urban is doing a set at the Country Music Hall of Fame," says Patrick, my scheduler. He pops into my office with one of his brilliant smiles. I stare up into the blinding whiteness of it all and swear I can count fourteen incisors, all perfectly buffed and photo ready.

Patrick and I have an agreement. He schedules something for me once or twice a month that falls into a "fun" category, thinking things like music and community theater will offset the endless meetings, late nights, and early mornings. Patrick loves the "fun" category. He and his gorgeous boyfriend, William, sometimes join me when something falls into the "especially fun" category.

"You can bring a plus-one," he says, smiling again. "Do you think Bruce would like to go?"

Not unless a surviving member of the Grateful Dead will be there too, I think.

Patrick and I have never talked about Bruce, but we don't need to. Patrick plans my days. He knows who's with me, and he knows who's not.

"Bruce won't want to go, but you can ask him if you want," I say.

"You want me to ask him?" Patrick says. The smile gets even more cheerful.

"No. It's okay. I'll text him," I mutter.

His smile droops along with his optimism that somehow Bruce will rally and surprise us both.

I pick up my phone and text, just to prove it to myself.

> I think Keith Urban is doing a set at the Hall of Fame later. I have a plus-one. You're welcome to join me!

He texts back:

> Do you need me to go?

I breathe deep and look out the window, watching the bureaucrats and lawyers shuffle in their loafers across the thick skin of frost outside the courthouse.

I should say, "Yes, I need you to go" or "Yes, I want you to go." But I don't.

I write:

No.

He writes back in a nanosecond:

I'll pass.

I close my computer and look up at my doorway. Rob is there, looking like he just stepped out of a Brooks Brothers ad.

• • •

February starts slowly, and I have time to think. I think mostly about secrets. I wonder how long Rob could keep his hand on mine without flinching, or if he'd ever tell anyone if he decided to leave it there for a while. He's good at keeping secrets. It's part of his job, and judging by how successfully he's screwed around on his wife, it might even be a bit of a hobby. I ran on transparency, and I believe in it, but I've never had anything to hide before.

Bruce's birthday party is at Skull's Rainbow Room, a wonderfully sordid, perfectly tacky burlesque joint in Printer's Alley with a prohibition-style mahogany bar and good fucking cocktails. It's our place, close enough to Broadway to sop up the occasional pickled tourist, but spiritually far, far away from the razzle dazzle of the honky-tonk machine. Skull's is where Nashville goes to slip out of her Bible belt and shake her ass a little, and we love it here, even though my detail always whisks me away before anything remotely risqué happens.

Twelve of us meet there. Bruce doesn't have a ton of friends. Friends wear him out, so I let him borrow mine for occasions like this, which suits everyone fine. I get a table in the back, not far from the stage, where a jazz singer adjusts her heavily sequined dress and gets ready to sing Billie Holiday and Etta James. Jamie, the piano player, is warming up, leaving his sheet music in a stack on the floor and letting his hands remember the music. The room is dark and sexy; it smacks of everything that used to be forbidden, strong drinks and dancing girls, $50 prime rib and infidelity. The black-and-white-checked floor is mostly empty, playing host to exactly one dancing couple, who, by the look of it, started drinking around 10 AM. We shake our heads and watch them, making our crotchety old jabs about tourists and pedal taverns and bachelorette parties, and the slow, humiliating death of old Nashville. Of course, everyone around the table threatens to call the mayor. It's the kind of conversation Bruce would love, but he isn't here. He left yesterday afternoon for a work trip to New Orleans.

We're having his birthday party without him.

I might've known if we spent more than forty seconds a day in conversation. I might've known if I'd checked his schedule like Patrick always tells me I should. But I didn't.

The booze hits fast and hard, which at the end of a long week is fine by all of us. We laugh until we're gasping, and we eat too much. Vodka martinis and wine shine bright and red across the table, and I relax into a musky state of bliss that I inherited from my father. I start to feel bold and a little reckless.

Rob is on my detail; he's standing diligently against the wall, a comfortable distance away from our drunk, shit-slinging conversations.

Things with Rob and me have gotten personal. Things *do* get personal when you spend fourteen hours a day with someone. Rob knows how I take my coffee and that I wanted to be a journalist when I grew up. I know that he joined the police department back when they tried to make bad cops out of good cops. I imagine he landed somewhere in the middle. We became friends, but we didn't stay friends very long. Soon his breath was falling heavier on my cheek when he whispered the name of a CEO in my ear, and he lingered long enough that my knees shook. I spent extra time getting ready in the morning; every item of clothing I put on was a strategic message to Rob of the skin underneath. I played coy, and he played dumb. Our little games started off so innocent, but only because we don't have enough time to play them the way we wanted to. The colder it's been getting, though, the longer it's been taking me to get home at the end of the night.

When he picks me up in the morning, our days begin in February of 2016 but end somewhere in July of 1981, just two kids driving around listening to '70s rock who know every single guitar riff and every single word. We talk about nothing important, but everything true: summer concerts, old boyfriends and girlfriends, frat parties, and first times. What I wouldn't give for a few more first times.

One day I asked him to guess my favorite song by the band Heart. He scrawled something on a slip of paper that he keeps in his breast pocket and slid it across the console. I met his hand with mine and let it stay long enough to play sexual chicken, each of us wordlessly daring the other to stay a little longer and a little longer. I peeked at his message, a note from the bad boy three lockers down.

"All I Want to Do Is Make Love to You."

He got it right, in more ways than one. The intimacy that turned to desire turned to lust, and every few days he kept reminding me that he was fabulous at having and concealing affairs.

"I'll never confess," he has assured me. "I'm good at keeping secrets."

I wonder if I could keep a secret too.

"Come sit with us," I say, signaling him to leave the wall and join us.

He puts a hand up and smiles, looking over, and his eyes travel the distance of my legs.

"I'm fine," he says, but it's the wrong answer for a group of upper-middle-class scallywags having a party. Graciously, they start in on him, so I don't have to.

"Oh, Rob! Please!"

"Get over here, buddy!"

"There's a chair for you!"

There isn't a chair for him, though. There's a chair for Bruce.

It doesn't take much more prodding. Rob pulls out the seat next to mine, and without the Tahoe's console there to make sure we leave room for Jesus, our legs find each other immediately.

On the way home, we say nothing. We said it all in hand resting next to hand under the table, in fingers slowly climbing fingers. Neither of us flinched.

The Tahoe doesn't even slow down when it passes my empty house. We go past the tree Max used to climb when he was ten, past the overflowing recycling bin that Bruce put out before he left for the airport so I wouldn't have to worry about it. Rob pulls up to the cross street and finds what feels like the darkest corner of the darkest parking lot in Nashville. He looks at me, and we're both seventeen again. I don't know what happens after he puts the Tahoe in park; I only know how I feel: free.

Long after he drops me off at home and heads to his home in Hermitage, Tennessee, I still feel his lips climbing my jawline. The things he whispered and the way he whispered them echo from my ears to the edges of my body. I fall onto the bed, humming the last few lines of Bob Seger's "Beautiful Loser" until the dogs and I finally find sleep.

Just a Little Weed

I'm looking through a forest of college-aged torsos and into a glass case filled with muffins that have been aggressively studded with chocolate chips and wrapped in fancy brown paper. Fido, our local coffee shop, is slammed. It's normally busy because they make a good breakfast sandwich, but today it's because Hillary Clinton is here, walking toward the counter, approximately three steps in front of me.

The coffee date is her team's idea. As Donald Trump plows his way through modern civilization like one of those pie-eyed cartoon steam engines, my popularity continues to grow. I'm a darling of liberal politicians, a historic first, the antidote to hypernationalistic Southern machismo cropping up on the fringes. I'm definitely a bright spot in the news cycle. Hillary appearing with me is a good thing, for her campaign, the coffee shop, and democracy. In the Mid-South, my endorsement matters, and I'm with her in the pursuit of liberty, justice, and caffeine.

"Hi!"

"Hello."

"It's so nice to meet you."

We comb slowly through the tangle of bodies, and I try not to be totally staggered by the number of eighteen-year-olds who recognize us. Finally, someone from Hill's team reaches the register and orders. Don't worry, I'm careful to only call her "Hill" in my head.

I get a latte and decide against hoovering a muffin in my good suit. She settles on a local medium roast, black.

Why didn't I order a local medium roast, black?

I'm immediately self-conscious that her coffee order is cooler than mine.

There's a rush of flashbulbs and cameras and camera phones. Her security team whisks her out back and into the shiniest SUV I've ever seen. After a few more handshakes, I follow. Rob ushers me over to the Tahoe. We'll go to Fisk University for the rally and then to my old friend Opponent A's house for Hill's fundraising event. Opponent A and I have had our issues, but Ted Danson and Mary Steenburgen are going to be there, so no issue is too big. Plus, he won't skimp on the catering. It's twenty-five grand a ticket.

When we turn onto Twenty-First Avenue and away from the press, Rob grabs my hand.

"You look beautiful today," he says with a smile.

I smile back.

• • •

At first, it isn't an affair. It's a series of unrelated chemical reactions between two lonely people in the same car, two people who feel unloved and uncertain as to where the past twenty years went. But as spring unfurls itself, we become something different. Sharing a secret becomes trust. Trust becomes friendship. Friendship becomes whatever this is, an alternate reality where we're the small-town boyfriend and girlfriend from the shitty John Mellencamp song and not coworkers fucking our way through our respective midlife crises. I like being with him. He makes me feel *not* lonely.

It's a Tuesday at 8 AM in March. Rob turns the Tahoe into a cemetery off Fourth Avenue. It isn't a place I've visited before, but I recently saw it on an episode of *Nashville*, a nighttime soap on CMT with fabulous music and theatrical Southern accents. I'm still catching up, but Scarlett's absentee mother just died of a brain aneurysm while trying to donate part of her liver to alcoholic Deacon (who also has cancer). They're making peace with the tragedy by naming a bar after her. As one does.

"It's pretty," Rob remarks, before driving through the iron gates. *Pretty* is a typical Rob adjective, along with *great* and *good*. The simplicity doesn't bother me. I never have to wonder how he's feeling.

"It *is* pretty," I say back. He smiles at me. He always likes it when we agree on a thing. I like how easy it is to make him happy.

A plaque in the median proclaims this as the "city cemetery," the oldest continuously operating public cemetery in town. Fifteen of Nashville's mayors are buried here. It's a perk of the job. If you're a mayor, you get a free plot. Lucky me.

Rob turns the radio to Sirius XM, the Bridge, and we drive the narrow lane that is lined on either side with a variety pack of Southern trees—magnolias and elms, crepe myrtles and weeping willows. The lawn is filled with elaborate structures—obelisks, box tombs, tabletops—all in granite and marble. "Hot Blooded" by Foreigner comes on. Obviously, it's the wrong crowd.

The lane dumps into a small parking lot, just big enough for four cars, and the road splits left and right, making a circle through the twenty-acre site. Rob slows down, but I ask him to keep driving. I roll down the windows to breathe in the morning air, which is warm and full of nectar. I have my first State of Metro speech in a few hours.

Rob reaches over and takes my hand. "I love that you wanted me to bring you here. I came here as a kid in school. I haven't been back since."

We are at the beginning, where each morsel of his life is fascinating. I want to know how old he was when he came here and why, what color his hair was, if he had a dog, a paper route, a best friend. I'm lustful about it; I ask and ask and ask.

He makes a slow turn to the right and we inch our way past more graves, into a part of the cemetery that's stark. The graves here have eroded and are in greater need of repair. There are large stretches of grass with no clear markers. He asks me about my life too.

I tell him about why I had to go to the Catholic girls' high school and I tell him about my dad, who was devoutly gay but raised Catholic.

"Wow," he breathes, eyes (probably) wide behind his most Secret Service–esque sunglasses. "That must have been tough."

He's listening.

I love that he's listening.

I love that he's simple.

I love that he's here.

The road gently bends back. It's almost time to head to the office. Warm spring weather has made the Bradford pears burst with white blooms, and they're falling in heavy clusters onto the asphalt.

"Almost forgot," he announces, stopping midway along under a shower of petals.

He hands me the daily schedule. Three pages of crisp white paper, front and back, neatly spelling out every minute of my day. I remember again who I am, what I do, where I belong. This is not "Jack & Diane."

"At least it's not a late night," I say. I laugh as I look at the day parceled out into color-coded blocks. "Looks like I'm home by 9:00."

We veer to the left, completing the circle.

"Can you stop for a second?" I ask. "I need to just breathe."

He puts the Tahoe into park, and I step outside, into the sweet and sour smell of the pears and springtime. We're in front of the monument to William Carroll, a former governor. A muscular eagle is perched at the top, with outstretched wings, the pectorals of a WWE wrestler, and a wide-open beak. There's a soldier's helmet carved into the middle of the stone above the epitaph. It's one of the bigger memorials and abundantly American. I run my hand over the coolness of the granite.

"Do you think he had any say in this before he died?" I ask Rob. "I mean, you have to wonder about that."

Rob cocks his head and makes brief eye contact with the eagle.

"Was he an asshole?" I go on. "Did he have a huge ego? Did he say, 'Make my monument the biggest and adorn it with a whole lot of military shit'? Who knows?"

I laugh.

Rob is quiet.

My stomach sinks. This is a Bruce conversation. The kind of thing he'd talk about for days and write about in one of the weeklies *if* he was still allowed to do that. I pivot.

"How about you?" I ask. "Do you have someplace picked out for when you die?"

"Yes," he says in a voice just above a whisper. "Sheri and I have plots together. That's where I'll be buried."

'Til death do us part is thinking small, I guess. I shove my hands in the pockets of my blazer, bracing myself as a momentary coolness passes over us. It comes and goes quickly.

"We should go," I say to him.

He rubs his index finger along mine and smiles. "You're going to do great today. You look nice and your speech is really good."

And in an instant, I forget about love. I forget about death. I absorb my complimentary one-syllable adjectives and go to work.

My State of Metro address *is* "really good" and by all accounts so is the state of metro. The Three-Year Action Agenda we rolled out to address the traffic issues is, even in its infancy, beginning to make a quantifiable difference and is projected to reduce traffic delays by nearly

25 percent. We're repaving the things people want repaved and adding sidewalks and bike lanes. We're moving forward on a bold comprehensive transit plan, and we've engaged the community to help design it. We're making a difference in people's lives.

. . .

Max comes home from school in April for the spring break practically catatonic. He's not taking care of himself. He's taken to wearing the same T-shirts that his dad does, only in white, and with large swishy basketball shorts instead of blue jeans. He hardly talks to us. The whites of his eyes are tinged pink and gluey-looking, and he lumbers around the house like a twenty-one-year-old grizzly bear. Graduation is next year, and he has no plans or employment prospects. He says he might like to go to Colorado, which is not a career path but just another state where he can get stoned without getting a ticket. I've been trying to set him up for success with internships, summer job opportunities, and meetings with local leaders in the fields that interest him. Or, the fields I want to interest him—journalism, education, communications. It hasn't gone over well.

"What the fuck, Max?" I ask one morning. He's rummaging around the refrigerator for leftover anything. He's been with us three days and bailed on two events and a meeting with Dave, a good friend who has told me he'll hire him, if Max will just meet with him.

"Don't you have an interview today?"

He sighs, which I take to mean "I heard you, but will continue to deny your existence."

Light is blaring through the window. He winces at it.

Max needs a plan. I need for Max to have a plan. He's been on the other side of the country for the past three years, so his diet of petrified

Domino's and bong water hasn't been an issue. Once he's back here, living under a microscope, it will be. He's going to ruin his future.

What the fuck happened? Max was a good kid. He played Little League and did fine in school. He made friends easily and let us mark his height on the doorjamb and take his picture on the first day of school for thirteen straight years. Barring the time he was the look-out for some friends who lit a puddle of antifreeze on fire outside the MAPCO, he stayed out of trouble. He's unquestionably in trouble now.

"Max?" I ask again.

He doesn't hear me, or he won't. I drum my nails on the countertop and try to look demonstrably angry, a move that sails right by him.

Boldly, he lifts the top of a cloudy-looking Tupperware dish and sniffs before moving on to a suspicious mass of foil. He's on something.

I call Sean and tell him to cancel the interview for a possible communications internship.

"Max can't make it today," I tell him.

"Is everything okay?" he asks. This is Sean at his most tender. As a rule, he doesn't get too personal. I think this is so he can retain the ability to be mean to me, which I need and am grateful for.

"Yeah, he ate something," I half lie. It isn't true yet, but the way he's eyeing the tower of Styrofoam containers behind the mayonnaise, it's about it to be.

"Tell . . . I'm sorry. I'll call to reschedule later today."

But I know I won't.

I need to fix this, and I need Bruce to do it.

• • •

Bruce is outside on the side porch listening to the Mets on his radio when I decide it's time for our Max conversation. Boris and Hank are lying at his feet thwacking their tails against the rotting wood. We have Comcast, but Bruce doesn't believe in baseball on TV. I choose my approach carefully and sit next to him on an uncomfortable steel patio chair, pretending to listen along.

The commentator is talking about Michael Conforto, the out-fielder. Bruce is rapt.

"We need to do something about Max," I say gently. "He needs to find something he likes. He doesn't have any direction."

I'm trying to convey a sense of powerlessness and desperation; I'm playing the kitten in the tree. Bruce isn't buying it.

"He's fine, Megan. He just doesn't like what you like." He shrugs, leaning away from me and into the speaker.

Heavy conversations have never been our forte, and anything about Max tends to dissolve into shame and resentment quickly. To Bruce, Max can do no wrong. He wore a Grateful Dead T-shirt to the first day of first grade, and since then, Bruce has trusted him almost entirely with his own destiny. I've traditionally been a little more wary.

"Did you see him, though? I mean really look at him? He's been hungover, or something, since he got here," I counter.

"You haven't even been here," Bruce shoots back, looking hate-ful, maybe for the first time ever. "We ate dinner together last night. He's fine."

What I would give for him to just say, "Fuck you, Megan."

I lean my head onto his shoulder, something I know he won't like but feel compelled to try anyway. He doesn't brush me off, but his whole body stiffens at the touch of mine. My hand is a hornet that's landed on his knee. He clears his throat and shifts.

"Max is fine. It's just a little weed."

I've done "a little weed." This is not that. I don't know what it is. I'm scared. And I'm alone.

"Do you think he's depressed?" I ask.

"Probably," Bruce says, eyeing me in a way that feels more biting and accusatory than it should.

I stand there looking back at him. A line drive smacks across Citi Field, and he fades into the game.

"I need to go to the office for something," I mutter. Rob meets me there.

• • •

Having the affair is not hard. Nobody suspects a thing, even though I walk around smelling like I've been showering in aftershave. Politicians across America have been fucking the people they work with for decades, but those are men. Rob's famously paranoid wife (who is actually not paranoid and is, in all instances, other than this one, highly observant) hasn't even batted her perfect lashes. Around others, Rob and I are professional. We don't mess with work. There is a clear separation between Rob the bodyguard and Rob the guy I sleep with occasionally. It's a practical arrangement. The boundaries are clear. Bruce doesn't suspect a thing either.

Rob's hand is fighting its way up my pencil skirt. We're in the underground parking garage of the Metro Courthouse. It's a Sunday and nobody else is here. He's telling me I'm beautiful and great and good. Occasionally, he tries to talk dirty but defaults quickly to niceties, which I prefer anyway because I don't like the way he stumbles over the word *pussy*.

Victoriously, Rob reaches the Spanx. He should be asking who wears Spanx on a Sunday.

They'll keep him busy for a little while, I think, and let my mind wander.

It's my sister Heather's sixth birthday, which makes me nine, and we have a '67 gold Lincoln Continental with suicide doors. My sisters and I are fascinated by the doors. They swing the wrong way and make people look at us in the Milgram's parking lot. Mom decorates the car with balloons and streamers and calls it the "birthday mobile" and arranges to pick up my sister's friends for her party. She retrieves seven little girls and brings them all back to the house for pizza and pin the tail on the donkey.

We all gather hungrily around the table. Dad is bringing home pizzas.

"He'll be here any minute," Mom sings out.

We wait. I can see her becoming increasingly angered by the lack of pizza. Luckily, my sister and her friends are distracted by the ancillary birthday games my mother has arranged.

She slams the white pages out and begins flipping through to find names and places. A moment later, she punches numbers into the phone.

"Is he there?"

She punches more numbers.

"Is he there?"

Again.

"Is he there?"

I peer across the table and see just enough to register that she's calling bars.

"Is Daddy an alcoholic?" I ask.

She shoots me a look and turns back to dialing. Nobody has seen him.

Dad arrives home, several hours late, looking disheveled and glassy-eyed. He's carrying the pizzas for the party, but the little girls were ferried home in the birthday mobile hours before. I'm still sitting at the kitchen table and, as always, happy to see him. My mother is not. He smiles cheerfully at us, trying to jolly her out of her displeasure. This is what Dad does when Mom pulls her shit—the accusations, the buzzkill, and reminding him he's a father.

"Ask him the question you asked me earlier, Megan." This is what Mom does when Dad pulls his shit—the lateness, the lying, and forgetting the birthday party.

Fuck, I think.

"Ken, I want you to hear what your daughter asked me when you didn't show up. Ask him," she says.

I'm mortified. This is the last thing I want to do.

"It's okay, Megan. You can ask me. What do you want to know?" Dad says, brightly, his brown eyes focusing on mine.

"When we were waiting on the pizzas and Mom was looking for you, it looked like she was calling bars to find you. Are you an alcoholic?" I ask.

She doesn't give him time to answer. "Your kid thinks you're an alcoholic, Ken. Isn't that funny? Go on. Answer her. Are you?"

He sighs a forever-long sigh through his nose.

"No, Megan, I'm not." I watch his eyes go from a wilderness to a prison in a single second.

I run upstairs, slamming my bedroom door as I hear Mom laugh and shout afterwards.

"He's not an alcoholic," Mom yells after me. "He's something much, much worse."

So am I.

• • •

Max heads back to school to finish out the rest of the year, which is a relief. I'm having more concerned "How's Max?" conversations in the Kroger than I'd like. Our neighbors are mostly discreet, but it's the South, where gossip is practically its own language. Bruce keeps telling me Max is fine, but I'm no longer placated by it. The mayor's son should be better than fine. The mayor's son should make a positive impact. He should be a leader. The mayor's son shouldn't sit around the house roll-ing joints with his friends and listening to Snoop Dogg.

I try to spin Max all on my own, by building a youth employment initiative called "Opportunity Now," which I say was inspired by my son and young people like him. Kids preparing to enter the job market gain access to paid job training and apprenticeships. Banks help them learn to manage their finances. It's a coup. The team is thrilled. The press is thrilled. Even the Republicans like it. Everybody wins. People are talking about Max's program, not Max's problem.

In Nashville's eyes, I can't seem to lose, but I'm losing everything.

Vice President, Student Body

Student Government Elections, Notre Dame de Sion School for Girls, 1979

Megan Mueller: 22 votes

Nicole P.: 146 votes

At sixteen, I run against Nicole at the Notre Dame de Sion School for Girls, where I've been sent to finish out my high school experience. I'm no longer in the public school system, which apparently is populated with what my parents have decided are "bad influences," and where I have spent my entire educational life. Instead, I'm among the cloistered, blue-skirted, virginal teens, who giggle at *Playgirls* in English class and cheat in chemistry by writing formulas on long erasers and passing them furtively during exams. I have to go the Catholic girls' school because I am a rebellious, shitty teenager who is making my parents' and sisters' lives miserable as hell.

Since there are no boys available, the nuns at Notre Dame de Sion let us play government, which is nice but hard to call a step forward since we're still not allowed to wear pants here.

Mom tells me, "You can be anyone you want at this new school," as she eyes my Bo Derek white girl braids and my double-pierced ears. I put on a white button-down shirt and leg warmers and run for vice president.

Nicole is going to upgrade the smoking area in the seniors' lounge and bring better lunch options to the vending machines. Her hand-drawn "Nicole 4 Vice President" posters hang all over the school and feature giant leaves of iceberg lettuce that look like dragon scales and fat wedges of tomato, so that we all know she's not fucking around about lunch. I don't have any posters. Or a platform.

I walk into the gym the day of the election and feel something, an electricity, an excitement cutting through the piousness and the sweat that permeates the whole building. The girls are chatty and engaged, sitting neatly on the bleachers and under the watchful eye of the Jesus crucifix hung over the door. He normally only presides over girls' basketball games, so this will be a big thrill for all of us.

Sister Stephanie walks up to the microphone and welcomes us, introducing Nicole and me and thanking us for preparing our speeches. I don't have anything prepared. Of course, I want to win, but I'm banking on my reputation as a cool new kid with double-pierced ears to get me through, not my agenda.

Nicole approaches the lectern and smiles a very white smile. Her teeth are perfect, like piano keys. I have a vague recollection that her dad might be a dentist and once gifted the school four hundred Oral-B toothbrushes. The only thing my dad could gift the school is ketchup packets from the bar and maybe a venereal disease, also from the bar. By now, I'm starting to understand the arrangement. Four nights a week, he's allowed to go out. The other three nights, he's stuck repenting like the rest of us.

Nicole is going on and on about butter-flavored croutons and shredded carrots. She spouts out facts about the importance of vegetables, nutrition, and academic performance. Nicole has priced out the salad, she has spoken to the administration about salads, and she has plans to donate unused salad to the homeless shelter at the end of each day. As she speaks, there is a concerning amount of nodding. When she's done, there is a concerning amount of applause, for which Sister Stephanie has allotted thirty seconds.

With a pristine smile, Nicole returns to her seat beside me and says, "Good luck," squeezing my bare knee with a sweaty hand. I stand up and walk to the lectern, looking down and noticing that the T-shirt underneath my button-down is completely visible. It has "Coca-aine" instead of "Coca-Cola" emblazoned across the breast. The microphone picks up my heavy breathing when I'm still a couple of feet away.

"Hello! My name is Megan Mueller," I say. I smile, but my teeth are closer to the color of vanilla bean from Zarda's Dairy.

Two hundred and ninety pairs of eyes turn to meet mine, but I have nothing to say to them. No plans. No vision. No salad. Just rambling.

I tell them that I'm enjoying the school. I believe in the school . . . And Jesus. I believe in Jesus. I love Jesus.

Oh Jesus.

Puddles of sweat underneath my arms and between my breasts grow with every nonsensical word I say.

"Any questions?" I lob in there at the last second.

There are no questions. There is no question. Nicole has it in the bag. Nobody gives a shit that I'm cool; they want salad and plans and someone who's thought it through. My face hot with mortification, I jog from the lectern straight out into the hallway. I don't lose because I couldn't do the work. I lose because I didn't.

I find an open stall in the bathroom and light a cigarette. Being vice president probably would have sucked anyway.

Bush League

Max wants tickets to the Sounds game. We're only about an inch into summer, but it's already ninety degrees. Everything is covered in a film of pollen and sweat. A soft haze hangs over the city, giving halos to the trees and buildings. It's like looking through a pair of smudged reading glasses. Small pearls of sweat collect on my upper lip and neck. I feel gross. I wish I'd worn my hair up.

The Sounds are Nashville's AAA baseball team, an affiliate of the Oakland A's. We're playing the Round Rock Express from Round Rock, Texas, who I'm told are better than us. Nashville is more of a football town, but everyone loves the Sounds because the tickets are cheap and they play in a stadium with a Jumbotron shaped like a child's drawing of an acoustic guitar. The facility is brand-new, and the city overspent on it.

People in stiff, just-purchased hats and team T-shirts, unwashed and brightly colored, are waiting in the line at the box office. I'm standing with them and so is Big Steve, my security detail for the evening.

"Ouch!"

Steve swats at a mosquito. I watch him look down at the mess of blood and crushed bug on his hand with a look of deep offense and shock. He's built like a mastodon and gentle as a lamb. I like him.

The line moves quickly. Even though I'm dressed like everyone else, in a hot, itchy jersey, people recognize me, mostly because I have a nine-foot-tall security officer next to me. They smile and wave. Everyone is in a great mood. I'm supposed to make an appearance on the field during the seventh inning at just about the time that everyone will decide to go to the bathroom or get that last beer. I buy twenty tickets for Max and his friends. He's thirty minutes late.

Steve and I walk back to the Tahoe to wait, leaning against the bumper and shooing the lightning bugs away. The lightning bugs are magical but fucking everywhere. I only stop shooing when I imagine the success a photo of Nashville's mayor swatting away the South's preeminent nighttime wonder would have on social media.

Max is now thirty-five minutes late.

Steve and I catch up. He hasn't been on duty much lately because he has a new baby at home, so Rob and I have been together a lot. The chief beefed up my security after a not entirely sober individual grabbed me and kissed me on Broadway. Apparently, nobody tried that shit with the previous mayor, Karl Dean. The rules are different for a woman, and nobody seems to know exactly what they are. Including me. Steve shows me a few photos of his tiny pink son in a onesie and miniature socks. He's a sweetheart, just like Max, who is now forty minutes late.

A Lyft pulls up and Max's body pours out. He's forty-five minutes late now.

"Momma!" he yells, clinging to the door of the driver's Nissan Sentra and struggling to get to his feet. Swaying, he looks down at the parking space between us like it's a fast-moving river. Steve gives me a look and helps Max over to the Tahoe. His pupils are the size of pinpricks, and he can barely stand up and smells strange and sick. He's wearing a white T-shirt and cargo shorts. Both are way too tight.

He burps loudly.

Fuck, I think. There are people everywhere.

"You're high. Get in the car," I say.

He tries unsuccessfully to roll his eyes.

"I'm fine, Momma. Really, I'm not 'on' anything," he mumbles, making little quotation mark claws with his fingers.

"Get in," I tell him.

He sighs in agreement. Too out of it to navigate more conversation, he crawls into the backseat. I climb into the front.

I turn around, about to lose my shit on him, and he nods off.

"Well, what the fuck am I supposed to do now?" I ask no one, burying my head in my hands. I'm supposed to be playing catch with Booster the Rooster at the seventh-inning stretch, and my kid is passed out in the backseat.

"Ma'am," Big Steve says. Poor Steve. I forgot he was even here. I wish it was Rob. Then I wish it was Bruce.

"I don't think there's any way he can go into the stadium," Steve goes on. "It's a sold-out crowd tonight."

I'm sure what he wants to say is "You're the fucking mayor. Please don't take your completely stoned-off-his-ass kid into a place where there's a Jumbotron and ten thousand people judging you."

"You're right." I sigh, making small circles on my temples, trying to coax out a better solution. There isn't one. Bruce is out of town. Max is my problem.

"You need to take us home."

Shaggy dark hair fills the rearview and Max briefly looks up.

"Where we going? I thought game . . . Baseball," he slurs.

He shuts his eyes and his head knocks against the window, bobbling every time we brake. Occasionally he wakes up and mutters, "What, Momma?" and then in a moment of lucidity says, "Are you taking me home? Good. I didn't want to go to the game anyway. Let's just chill tonight. You and me. Dad's out of town, so it'll just be . . ." And then he nods out again.

What a mess.

"If I can just get him home, he'll sleep it off," I say with a grim smile. "The game would have been fun, but there's an upside—it means you get to knock off early, and you can go home and be with that baby. Can you let whoever might care know that I'm not going to make it tonight?"

"Of course, ma'am," Steve promises.

It'll be fine. Steve will say something nondescript, something that makes it all sound very serious but very handled. "The mayor is so sorry she can't be at the game. There was a family matter she had to attend to."

Really, everyone goes to the bathroom before the seventh inning anyway.

• • •

We pull up to our house and the lights in every room are blazing. Max clearly made a stop on his way home from the airport. I'm less than excited about the surprise bullshit I might find in there.

I'm pissed off and embarrassed. I spent the whole drive stewing.

"Max, wake up."

I do not say this gently and I'm out of the passenger side in an instant. I open Max's door before Steve can get to it.

"Wake up," I repeat, not prefacing the request with "fucking" but conveying it very clearly. I lean in to undo his seat belt. His skin is hot and clammy at the same time. His eyelids flicker. There's no recognition of me and his pupils are still flea sized.

"Do you need help getting him into the house? I *can* help," Steve says.

Max is much bigger than me and right now has the reflexes of a sloth.

"No, he can get his ass out of the car. Come on, Max," I say.

"Ma'am." Big Steve's voice quivers. I tell him he can leave, but he waits.

Max stumbles out onto the street and wobbles toward our gate. He pauses as he grabs onto the fence, swinging the gate open and crawling up the stairs. Steve follows, spotting him as he fumbles his way down the walkway and up onto the porch. He leans against the door as I rummage around for my keys.

"Thank you, Steve," I say. "I've got it from here."

Steve returns to the car and lingers for a bit like a dad who's just dropped his tween daughter off alone at the CoolSprings Galleria for the very first time.

The house smells like leftovers when I open the door. Max totters toward the couch in the family room and makes a landing (mostly) on the cushions. His breath is irregular, occasionally broken up by something between crying and laughter that confuses the dogs, who have come to stare, lick their chops, and poke him in the neck with their wet noses. Aching, I bend down and wrestle with his white Nike tennis shoes, which are the size of carry-on luggage. I'm too angry to cry myself, but I want to. Here I am living my dream, looking down on my worst nightmare. *What the hell happened?*

Whatever *this* is, I feel responsible. It feels like it belongs to me. Max belongs to me.

My chest tightens and the tears come.

I'm filled with irrational, impossible love and a tenderness that's feral. All at once, I remember that I'm a mother. Every mistake I've made and forgotten—not being around enough, not being kind enough, not trusting him enough and then trusting him too much—washes ashore again. I touch his long, greasy hair and the patchy shadows of beard he missed while shaving. I tell him I love him and dab at the sweat collecting in the recess of his collarbone. *This is my baby.*

Suddenly, the quiet turns eerie. I'm not sure he's breathing.

"Max! Wake up!" His eyes open with a shock and shut again. He takes a big breath and slips back into unconsciousness.

"Max."

I pry an eyelid open. There's nobody home. His body lurches like it wants to vomit but can't.

Should I call an ambulance?

Max will be all over the news. His friends will know. His elementary school teachers will know. My voters will know.

Fuck.

I grab my keys from the drawer, and a wet dishrag, which I use like a spur, prodding and prodding. Miraculously, Max shivers to life.

"Momma?" he asks.

Thank God.

I sling his arm around my shoulder and brace for the weight of him.

"Where are we going now?"

"The hospital."

● ● ●

The Vanderbilt University Medical Center is about a half mile from our front door, a half mile that feels long and treacherous. I park my car on the U-shaped drive and try to rally Max. I can't. I don't know what to do.

Jogging to the entrance, I freeze at the threshold of the sliding door, which whizzes open and shut indecisively.

I catch the eye of the security guard.

"I need help. My son."

He nods. Within seconds, Max is being escorted, me on one side, security on the other. He nods in and out of the world, talking nonsense, strands of drool like spider silk falling from his lips to his chin to his shoulder.

We dump Max in a stained, pathetic chair that teeters a bit under him, and I head to the intake desk to give the necessary details. Thank God we have insurance. I spell out his name and birth date and do so as quietly as I can, lowering my voice when giving my name and avoiding eye contact with any potential constituents.

At the mention of "Megan Barry, mother," there is a sudden flurry of activity, and we are quickly escorted back behind a door. Max is taken into a separate room, and I am not allowed to go with him.

A nurse takes me to the second-saddest chair on earth in an area they've tried to make discreet with a thin curtain. They offer me either a small Styrofoam cup of water or a small Styrofoam cup of Sprite. I decline both. I'm glad to wait alone. Naïvely, I decide this VIP treatment is for my privacy, but I quickly realize that they're just trying to remove any possible agents of chaos from their already chaotic emergency department. They don't need press here. Neither do I.

"Can I talk to the doctor?" I ask the nurse with the drinks. She has a nose ring and a flash of blue hair under her ponytail.

"Not yet," she says with a cheerful and rehearsed grin, which she has probably used forty thousand times a shift in response to that exact question. "But someone will be in soon."

She disappears and I wait, adrenaline draining from my body as I thumb my way through a dog-eared and sticky issue of *Southern Living*. I try to like it, but it's mostly gingham and slow cookers.

Around midnight I call Bruce, who is in Colorado. He's shocked. I'm quietly indignant. I tell him not to come home, but of course I want him to ignore me and hop on a plane immediately. He doesn't. He had said Max was just smoking "a little weed." But he was wrong. Max was gaslighting both of us. Bruce couldn't handle the situation. And I wouldn't handle it. We just wanted it to go away. Shortly after, a doctor knocks on the wall and peeks in at me from around the curtain.

"Mayor Barry?"

I nod yes. *Great. He knows who I am.*

"Good news. Max is stable. You can pick him up around 6 AM. Everything should be out of his system by then."

I'm relieved. So relieved.

"Thank God. Thank *you*. What happened? What is he on? What do we do next?" I ask.

We can get ahead of this, I think. If Max needs rehab, we'll get him into rehab, quickly and *quietly*.

The doctor frowns.

"I'm sorry, but I can't tell you anything else. Max is an adult. He declined to sign the paperwork allowing us to share his medical information with his family members."

"But . . ." I'm hoping this one word will express that I'm the most powerful woman in the city, so he better give me something. I've been put in a curtained room after all.

"I do want you to know that Max doesn't seem very happy to be here," he warns. "He's let us know several times that he'd like to leave."

No shit. I'm not very happy to be here either. There's a clumsy moment of silence.

"You can head home and pick him up in the morning," the doctor says again. "That's how long it'll take to clear all of this from his body. There's nothing else I can tell you."

He shakes my hand. His skin is hard, cold, and smooth, like stainless steel.

I leave the emergency room totally disoriented. There are no pamphlets or follow-up appointments. No explanations. No next steps.

A lightning bug stalks me in small cheerful circles as I walk toward the car. I swat at it, and I don't fucking care who sees.

● ● ●

Heroin.

Mushrooms.

Overdose.

Kids. Drugs. Worst drugs.

Xanax.

Philip Seymour Hoffman death.

River Phoenix death.

I'm at home and all I can do is Google, like everyone else. I'm getting nowhere. I did a "Is Your Kids on Drugs?" quiz and read something in the *Atlantic* about decriminalization in Portugal. The internet can't answer any of the big questions anyway.

How did we get here?

Am I a good mother?

Why is he doing this to himself?

Delirious, I lay my head on the table and close my eyes. It stings. I retrace our steps, returning to the day Max was born, in the maternity wing of the same hospital he's in now.

"You can do it," a nurse says. I'm eight centimeters dilated. It doesn't seem like I have much of a choice whether I "do it" or not at this point. The pain is excruciating. I should have gotten the spinal block.

"We can take the edge off the pain a bit if you want and give you some Dilaudid," she suggests.

I nod. Yes, please. I don't know what Dilaudid is, but I'll do anything to make the pain stop. She adds something to my IV and instantly

I'm relaxed, swimming in my body. I'm euphoric. It doesn't hurt any-more. *Nothing* hurts. The contractions come faster.

"Bruce, this is the best high of my life," I say. "Tell them I want some more of this stuff when I'm finished."

He laughs.

Max H (no period) Barry is born at 7:52 PM. He's small, wheezy, and suffering from a birth injury on his head. They need to take him away for observation. He's little and helpless, with great hair. His cries are weak and ragged.

They place his small body in a glass Isolette, and as I watch him go, I hope the drugs in my system are coursing through his as well.

I don't want my baby to feel any pain.

I don't want my baby to feel any pain.

Emerald Cove

"Mississ-IPPI?!" Max's face is twisted into something between disbelief and disgust.

"Mississippi." He says it again, like it's a foreign food he's not willing to try, instead of the twentieth state to join the union.

Max has been home from the hospital for a few hours, and I've found him a bed at a rehab facility called River Glen outside Jackson. Despite the name, it's near neither river nor glen and is downwind from a Burger King and a Walmart Supercenter.

"You have to go, Max," Bruce says flatly. He's still in transit from Colorado, so I have him on speaker, and each time he talks I shove the phone toward Max, making him pay attention. Bruce and I appear united. We're projecting absolute certainty. Max is going to rehab. Max is getting clean. Everything is going to be fine.

"What about Emerald Cove in Tampa?" Max counters. "The place Joey went."

His friend's older brother went to Emerald Cove for rehab. Joey is still a fuckup. Plus, I'm not sending my kid to a place that so clearly evokes a bank of penny slots and a twenty-four-hour buffet, the kind with sneeze guards, pungent canned hollandaise, and sausages shaped like little gray cat turds. There's no goddamn way.

"You're not going to fucking Florida," I say.

Bruce agrees. He hates Florida as a matter of principle, and I follow "Florida Man" on Twitter, which highlights the state's sensational but true headlines.

"Florida Man Calls 911 to Report Lack of Vodka"

"Police Unable to Tow Florida Man's Illegally Parked Flintstones Car"

"Florida Man Proudly Claims He's the First Person Ever to Strap Six-Month-Old to Water Skis"

"Florida Woman Quits Job So She Can Breastfeed Her Boyfriend Full-Time"

I get the sense that they're spoiled for choice down there.

There are plenty of beds available in Tennessee, but it's too risky. Max can't be close to me right now. I don't want him close to me right now. We're way past a bad haircut and being grumpy about a prayer breakfast. Max is a liability. Politics runs on trust. People don't trust addicts and they don't trust the parents of an addict either. They'll hold me responsible. They always hold the parents responsible, especially the mother. I know. I've judged others in the past. If it gets out that Max is an addict, I become unreliable, shaky, unfit for the job. Suddenly, the woman running the city can't run her own household. It would be catastrophic, and the media would love it.

I imagine the headlines:

"Barry's Son, Out of Control, Rushed to Vanderbilt Hospital After Drug-Induced Episode"

"Mayor Barry Oblivious to Son's Addiction"

"Mayor's Drug-Addicted Son in Rehab at Emerald Cove, a Shitty Casino in Tampa"

Suddenly, I'm no better than Florida Man.

We haven't told anyone what happened. Sean is the only one from my team who knows, and in his perfect, discreet, Sean-like way, he has only brought it up as it concerns the office of mayor. Will I need time off? And if I do, what should we say?

Max takes a ragged breath and pulls at the collar of his T-shirt. He sounds like he might cry, but I know he won't. He's too proud, even with the hospital bracelet still hanging off his wrist. We all are.

"Whatever. Fine," he stammers, "I'll go."

I walk around the island and give him a hug. It's more businesslike than I want it to be. Bruce gives a giant sigh on the other end of the phone line.

It's been decided. Max is going to River Glen and he's going quietly.

Max takes the dogs for a walk, and I go upstairs to pack him a bag, refusing eye contact with all the perfect black-and-white family photos as I climb the steps. We look like Simon and Garfunkel album covers. I feel indiscriminately angry, tired, and staggered by the reality I'm living in. I know Max. Max is bad at baseball. Max calls his dad Pops. Max's left foot is slightly bigger than his right. I *know* him. Max isn't an addict.

But he is.

I love Max's room. It's bright and still adorned with a few hyper-masculine relics of boyhood—a bulletin board with a ski map of Breckenridge, stickers of snowboard makers on the wall, Colorado posters, *Hatchet* by Gary Paulsen, a nautical flag quilt with bright yellows and reds on the bed. I walk in and take inventory of the gold-painted plastic trophies (everyone gets one!) and several of his high school textbooks. *Wasn't he supposed to turn those in?*

Groggy and numb, I begin collecting white T-shirts, balling socks, and combing the back of his drawer for a zipper sweatshirt without strings, as strings are not allowed at River Glen. I paw around for the signs of trouble that I missed, peeking inside his baseball glove, his pillowcase, and his laundry basket for pills or pipes or a journal or a handle of whiskey, something. I shove the length of my arm under the mattress, reaching and waving, drowning and desperate. I'm looking for the keys to the fortress, for access to the person my son can't be but is.

We caught him smoking pot on the front porch in seventh grade once. Bruce and I were headed downtown to catch Roger Daltrey at the Ryman and Max called us eight times on his new cell phone to "just check in." We turned the car around and found a pipe thrown into the bushes.

I also found a stash of buds when he was in high school. The skunk smell emanating from his room had made me sniff his tennis shoes first, hopeful that he just needed a new pair, before discovering a jar of greenish weed in his dresser.

I knew he was stressed at college last semester and had started taking some anxiety meds.

He came home drunk just once, vomiting all over the bathroom floor, and had a two-day hangover.

And he smoked pot (along with the rest of Tacoma).

I knew something was off, different, but not this.

I find nothing. No answers.

Satisfied with the number of shirts and shorts but nothing else, I zip up the duffel and leave, shutting the door behind me.

Later that day, I give Max $200 for gas and emergencies. I hand him his bag and a box of pepper jack Cheez-Its. He holds Hank's jowls in his hands for a moment and slowly rolls his hands toward Hank's ears.

"You're a good boy," he assures him, voice quiet and almost pleading, like he wants him to say it back.

I give hugs and tell him to drive safely. A friend has agreed to drive with Max to Jackson. I'm not a hundred percent convinced they'll make it there, but it's the only way Max is willing to go. He tosses the bag in the back, throws a few Cheez-Its in his mouth, and waves with a smile. Then I watch the car disappear onto Hillsboro Pike, headed toward the interstate.

Bruce is still away. I catch him on his cell.

"He's gone."

"It'll be okay," Bruce says. "It'll be okay."

But he doesn't know that and neither do I. This is new territory. We don't know what we're doing. We don't even know what Max is hooked on. We just have to trust him.

• • •

That night, I get a call from Tampa just as I'm polishing off my second glass of wine.

"Mrs. Barry? This is Misty from Emerald Cove."

Misty sounds more like a Marge, hard and raspy.

"We wanted to let you know that your son, Max, arrived about an hour ago. We picked him up at the airport, and now we need a credit card and his insurance information to take care of everything before admitting him."

Fucking Max. He didn't go to Mississippi.

"Of course," I sing back to her. I'm "twinkling" again because the alternative is screaming.

"He went to Florida," I say out loud, to no one in particular. "Fucking Florida."

"It's a Visa," I say into the phone, before rattling off my credit card number to Misty/Marge.

"Perfect," she says flatly. "A Visa?"

No, Misty, it's a rocket ship.

I assure her again that, yes, it's a Visa, and then end the call as quickly as possible.

Max sleeps with his dog at the foot of the bed. Max loves Colorado. Max loves his longboard and his CRV. Max plays *Grand Theft Auto* and watches the Tennessee Titans. He knows all the *Seinfeld* references and has the same quirky sense of humor as his dad.

But I don't know Max at all.

I bury myself in the things I do know: work and Rob.

. . .

Blue lights swirl and a short, kind of casual siren blurps a few times, enough to indicate importance but not emergency. Traffic around Public Square stops, and Rob backs the Tahoe into the car bay on the back side of the courthouse. The garage door blends into the granite and is barely noticeable to passersby. This is how I come and go to the office every morning. Through the secret garage door we call the Batcave.

We maneuver into our parking space and Rob turns off the car lights. The sunlight is gone. We are engulfed in the solitude and dank parking garage smell, the hazy artificial glow from overhead.

I pull the side passenger mirror down to adjust my makeup as the garage door lazily closes. It's a Wednesday morning, around 7:15 AM.

Rob reaches over, takes my hand, and leans in to kiss me. I let him. I don't say anything about Max.

"Hello, beautiful," he purrs, tucking my hair behind my ear.

"What do we have on the schedule today?" I say, in as sexy a way a person can say something like that.

The secret of our affair has been painfully easy to keep. Nobody bats an eye if Rob follows me into my house when Bruce is away. It's his job to be close to me. The closer he is, the happier everyone seems to be. He's keeping me safe! I feel like I've practically been handed a pack of Trojans and some mood candles.

He hands me the neatly folded pages from his inside pocket, also trying to be sexy about it. Rob's long fingers gently brush against my blouse as he leans in closer. I'm trying to stay focused, but the heat of his touch is enough to dumb my sense of time and place. I want more because I want to forget.

The light above the interior stairwell door trembles and a fast-moving shadow plays underneath. I jump and glance over for a moment. I'm sure no one can see us through the car's tinted windows, but it isn't worth the risk. I unbuckle my seat belt and hop out, just in case. Rob comes quickly around and beats me to the door, pressing me up against the subterranean coldness of the wall, grabbing my breast hard through my shirt. He takes my chin in his hand and gently uses his tongue to open my lips. I have a meeting in five minutes.

"Later," I whisper, "when we have more time."

"Please, Megan."

He sounds like a little boy, begging.

"No. I can't. It's too risky. There are people right on the other side of the door. They might hear us."

His breath is wet and minty. We kiss again and he pushes himself into me.

Yes, Rob, I'm aware that you have a penis and a gun, I think.

For some reason, he always expects the erect penis to be the element of surprise.

"We can't," I whisper. "It's time to go."

I notice I've gotten lipstick on the lapel of his new Dillard's suit. It's a brilliant shade of pink.

"You're going to need to take care of that," I say, pointing to the fabric.

"Damn it. How am I going to explain this to Sheri?" he whines.

Not my problem, I think to myself, and push him aside, opening the door and stepping into the lighted hallway. I love that none of this is my problem.

"Morning!" Sean grins at me, as I walk up the stairs and onto the landing of the second floor. His smile is the first one I see in the morning.

"Hey!" I say back. "Did you have a good night?"

"Yes," he responds, nodding. "You?" he asks a little more seriously. He isn't going to bring Max up, but in his way, he is letting me know I can.

"Yeah," I say back, "I think everything is going okay."

Like a good politician, I say nothing and everything.

I head to the conference room to meet with Rich, the COO, and Natalie, the finance director. Today I'm getting an update on the budget, a figure that seems astronomical at $2 billion, but won't get us very far. We inherited too much debt from a mayor who also inherited too much debt from a mayor (he probably inherited too much debt from a mayor too). Our population has been swelling at a rate of over 2.5 percent per year, every year, for the past decade. We're working hard on the horrendous traffic, but working on said horrendous traffic has caused horrendous gridlock, which people are also upset about. We need to find solutions we can afford, and we can't afford much. Thankfully, tourism is keeping us afloat. Nashville is currently the top destination in the country for bachelorette parties and pedal taverns, and I remind constituents to say thank you to Cami and her bridesmaids. They are helping to fund stuff we need. We can't cut spending, but we can spend smartly.

Natalie goes over the current state of affairs, and we guzzle our way through a mountain of coffee. With Natalie there is no bad news—there are "exciting challenges" and "possible barriers." When she's done with her presentation, I'm filled with confidence and optimism in our future. Natalie should probably be the mayor one day.

Patrick comes in next to fill me in on upcoming events. Pride is this weekend and our LGBTQIA+ population is still reeling from an attack at a nightclub in Orlando. The mayor's office will continue to show meaningful, unwavering support. We'll need to beef up security for the event this year to make sure people feel safe. I'll need to find something colorful to wear that doesn't make me look like a frumpy, middle-aged rainbow troll. After Pride is Independence Day. So far, all I know about that event is that we've got Sheryl Crow and a shit ton of fireworks. Nashville has a particular fondness for fireworks. We receive a high volume of complaints about those as well.

By lunchtime, I realize I haven't thought about Max all day. I've liked not thinking about him. Not replaying the events of the past week has been good for me. I need to stay busy.

"Patrick," I shout, "I changed my mind. I want to go to that thing at Coleman Park this weekend, after all. It's important."

I can't even remember what the thing is.

He shoots me a thumbs-up.

The more I do, the better I feel. I just need to focus on Nashville.

Complain about the fireworks. Call me when it rains and the potholes appear. Call me when we miss your street on recycling day. Not enough trees in your neighborhood? Call me. We'll plant some.

But don't call me if you're someone I love with my entire soul and you've got a problem I can't fix. Have some mercy.

Max texts Bruce and me around 4 PM. We haven't expected to hear from him for a month. He doesn't have regular access to his cell phone and still won't sign any paperwork allowing someone to clue us in on what's going on.

> They just took me to the hospital. I guess I had a
> seizure when I was detoxing. I love you momma and
> I want you to know I appreciate everything you do
> for me. I'm going to get better.

Bruce is immediately on the phone to Emerald Cove trying to piece together what the hell is happening now. By the end of the day, he is full of updates and wants to discuss them.

"He says he's feeling better, Meggie. The detox is working and he's going back to rehab after the hospital. I told him I would fly down and bring him home, but he wants to stay and finish the treatment."

I nod along, but I don't want to talk about it. Bruce is too late. There was a moment for togetherness, and it passed. Max is Bruce's jurisdiction now. Nashville is mine. I want him to handle it and then I want it to go away.

It should have been Bruce in the emergency room, not me. It should have been Bruce poking around Max's neck for a pulse, feeling for breath on the back of his hand, prying Max's eyelids open with his fingertips, and trying to find him somewhere in the yellowing abyss—not me. I told him I was worried about Max. He didn't listen. The moment of empathy for the brokenhearted, shell-shocked dad has passed. I'm mad. It's too late. We aren't in this together. We aren't in anything together. How did we get here? It doesn't matter. I'm making my own choices now.

I want to be touched.

I want to be beautiful.

I want to be loved.

I want to forget.

I don't want to wait a second longer and I don't have to. I spend July with my hand in Rob's, taking the long way to work, driving the loop at the oldest cemetery in Nashville, where one day, I'll be buried. Today, I feel comically alive, forever sixteen years old in summertime.

● ● ●

At the end of the month, Max "graduates" from Emerald Cove, whatever that means. I don't know if it means I can trust him. I don't know if it means I forgive him. All I know is that he's had over a hundred thousand dollars' worth of treatment and we're lucky as hell to have insurance. We did what we were supposed to do. We got him help, quietly.

I make up the bed in his room with fresh sheets and fold his laundry. The sheet billows down over the naked mattress, making a pleasant Tide-scented breeze. Breathing it deeply, I tuck the corners and drape a top sheet over the pillowtop, smoothing it perfectly flat. I have never made a bed with such precision and artistry.

This, I think, *is the kind of bed making that changes lives.*

At least, I hope it does.

After chopping at the pillows, I lie on top of the comforter and shut my eyes, inhaling the smells of boy and dog tangled tightly together in the blankets, too ancient to be dulled by the detergent of mere mortals. I blink a few times, hoping for the world to feel new. Looking up at the ceiling fan fixtures filled with dust and the skeletons of black flies, I feel sorrow rush over me. I can't fix this. In this room, I have a terrifying lack of power.

In this room, I cry, quietly.

The Only Path

Recovery is clean and quiet. Nashville never knows. Our neighbors and friends never know. We don't mention it to our families. Max completes his thirty days, and we pretend them away, which, as I tell myself frequently in the moments just before sleep, is in my son's best interest. Getting back to normal will be the best thing for everyone. In this version of normal, though, he'll be occasionally required to excuse himself to go piss in a small plastic container I can evaluate in the master bath for any trace of opioids. I still don't know exactly what he was on. But he needs to be off them, permanently. It's the only path forward.

There are small flashes of awareness, though. My eyes fall closed, the sounds of the city hum peacefully together, and my head melts into the pillow. My body jolts. I know it isn't going away. Max is an addict. Normal is gone.

When Max comes home at the beginning of August, life isn't normal; it's a picture we paint. Without ever discussing it, Bruce and I fabricate an air of "hunky-dory" and Rob and I cool off. Suddenly, the Barrys are Family 2.0. We catch the Saturday matinee at the Belcourt and go for walks in Dragon Park with the dogs. Max invites Tommy and Matthew over to play *Zelda* and eat frozen disks of pizza that make the house smell like an Olive Garden on fire. We drink coffee on the side porch (Max is allowed to have as much coffee as he wants), talking about the Mets, the heat, and things that are breezy and palatable. We don't talk about the seizures that sent Max to the hospital during his detox. We don't talk about what he was on, when it started, where he got it, and why. We talk about the orb weaver in the yard, watching her spit silk into an egg-shaped web that hangs in the boxwoods. She watches us back, equally impressed with her handiwork.

At the end of the month, we feel confident sending Max 2.0 back to Tacoma sober, for his senior year of college. We are all sure things will be different.

But then, Bruce and I are alone again.

I text Rob:

> I miss you.

Habits like these are so hard to break.

• • •

It's September. Rob and I have just pulled into the garage, which is slick with the glaze of late summer humidity. I pop a stick of shockingly minty gum into my mouth and pull down the visor mirror to deal with my hair, which looks startlingly similar to the backside of a rained-on golden retriever.

"I love you," Rob says.

It comes out of nowhere and he's not even looking at me. He's staring straight ahead into the dim halo of light around the stairwell door.

My eyes bulge. A sharp, peppery corner of the gum hits me in the back of my throat, making me cough xylitol and wintergreen. The gravel of his voice is still scraping in my ears.

Rob doesn't love me. He can't love me. That's not how this works.

I don't say anything. Instead, I get out of the car and pretend it didn't happen, but he pulls me into his chest and kisses me deeply, dipping me back slightly and staring into my eyes. From a distance, I'm sure we look like a drugstore romance cover, the kind where the title, the pirate man's muscles, and the pirate wench's tits are embossed and pleasant to the touch.

He searches my eyes for some trace of epiphany or awakening, the realization that "Yes! I love him too!"

I can't say it back.

I give him a long, wet, brazen kiss. He reaches behind me for a handful of ass, which I graciously allow.

"We should go in," I whisper, trying to sound like I'm not panicking while I am filled with panic. I don't have the bandwidth to lie to Bruce *and* Rob. I don't love him. Not loving each other is the whole point. This was never supposed to be real. But with three words, it suddenly is.

What a fucking mess.

• • •

The office is its usual whir and blur. Rob's eyes follow me as I feel a horrible pressure to be sexy while doing unsexy things like microwaving my coffee, assessing the condition of my orchid plant, and reading a newspaper, which is currently skeptical of me.

Sean and I meet about a bill I'm preparing to sign that will decriminalize the possession of small amounts of marijuana. Low-income and minority residents are disproportionately affected by the existing laws, and it doesn't make sense financially or socially for the city to continue to treat these kids like hardened criminals. Sean settles into the couch as much as Sean settles into anything. He's upped his dress since we came into office and is sporting a suit and a tie.

"I'm excited about this one," he chirps before opening his laptop.

I am not excited. I have thoughts about kids and drugs right now, thoughts I didn't have before the curtained hospital room and Emerald Cove.

"It's just a little weed." Bruce's words echo in my head. I think of Max. I think of the night in the ER, how worried I was, and then how angry.

I take a long drink of my seductively prepared coffee and remind myself: *This isn't about me and my big, ugly thoughts; it's about my voters and their thoughts.* I compartmentalize.

I'm good at compartmentalizing. I believe it's one of the stronger instruments in my mayoral tool kit. At work, I think about work and nothing else. When I'm at home, I think about Bruce, Max, the dogs, calling my sisters and my mom, and watering the yard.

Compartmentalizing also makes me excellent at having an affair. Until now. "I love you" has sent me over the edge. Love won't be put in a tiny box. Rob's compartmentalizing is starting to slip.

"The bill," I say to Sean, "is good, but it isn't perfect. I'm worried."

Mother-whose-son-just-got-out-of-rehab feelings aside, the document does need some work.

A person can still be charged with possession under state law; our ordinance just gives officers another option, *if* they choose it. In theory, it means more younger Nashvillians are forgiven for their transgressions, but in practice, it may not make the difference I hope it will. Nationally, tensions between police and Black communities are rising. Alton Sterling was murdered by police July 5 in Baton Rouge, and just the next day Philando Castile was gunned down in front of his girlfriend while reaching for his driver's license in suburban Saint Paul.

Trust in law enforcement, rightfully, is shaky. What if this gives the police too much decision-making power? The Metro Council voted overwhelmingly in favor of the action. Decriminalization is the right thing *if* it's done the right way.

Sean nods thoughtfully, drafting things in his head. He stands up from the couch and paces the length of the room.

"So what do I say about it?" I ask.

"Say it's a step forward?" Sean suggests.

"It's a step forward," I agree, hoping that it will be.

Sean heads back to his desk to write out a statement and Rob is waiting outside the door. He winks at me. I want my compartments back. I need to make a statement of my own.

● ● ●

That night, I'm having a meeting at Skull's with Todd, a former professional athlete. Rob is on detail. Todd is charming, handsome, famous, and built like a Kodiak bear. And he's one of the few men on earth who can wear too much cologne and get away with it. There's always been a bit of harmless electricity between us, and I fully expect that he has harmless electricity with most women he encounters. Bruce and I have hung out with him a few times, and of course, Bruce has been completely oblivious to and unthreatened by our friendship.

"Why are you meeting him?" Rob asks as we're walking from our parking spot to the bar. "Is it business related?"

He's jealous. He needs to not be.

"It might be," I shrug.

He doesn't like the answer.

Begrudgingly Rob opens the door for me, unable to disengage from his Southern roots, even when he's pissed off.

"Madam Mayor," Todd says with a laugh and a ridiculous bow.

He wraps me up in a big hug. I hang onto him like a kid climbing an oak tree out back.

Rob watches us from the corner of the room with his jaw clenched.

I throw back a vodka martini on a mostly empty stomach. At some point in the day, a spinach salad was dropped on my desk with a sad little bag of ranch dressing that I poked open with my index finger. The day got busy and I'm not sure if I ever even ate the thing. It shows.

Blood arrives in my cheeks and my chest, and I laugh too loudly at Todd's jokes, which are pretty good.

Rob shakes his head, almost undetectably. He searches for my gaze, but I've gone intentionally blind to him.

"You want to grab one more on Broadway, cowgirl?" Todd asks.

"Why not?" I say, laughing. "We've got the car. Rob!"

Obediently, he brings the car around, shooting me daggers when Todd climbs in next to him and starts messing with the radio.

We park just off Broadway and walk into Robert's, one of the few remaining honky-tonks in what is becoming three city blocks of Margaritavilles. It wouldn't be advisable for me to publicly acknowledge which Lower Broad bar is my favorite, but it's a three-way tie with the oldies—Legends, Robert's, and Layla's.

The band is on a break, which normally would disappoint me, but when Todd and I walk across the battered wooden dance floor, each of us taking time to smile and nod at those who recognize us, I twinkle up. I love being recognized. I'm not sure if I'm supposed to love it, but I do.

We find a table not far from the dance floor and Todd goes to the bar for us.

"I'll switch to bourbon," I call after him.

A place can't be famous for their fried bologna sandwiches and their vodka martinis at the same time. Bourbon is the better bet. I'm having fun and feeling free, something Rob used to evoke, and ages ago Bruce.

Some sorority girls from Vanderbilt approach the table and ask for a selfie. Rob grabs my arm. Hard.

"Mayor, you're drunk," he says through clenched teeth. "Let's go home."

I don't want to go, and I especially don't want Rob telling me what to do. He pulls me away from the girls, who have shifted their attention to just-returned Todd. They don't recognize him, but he is so unquestionably somebody, they get their selfie anyway.

"I'm not going yet," I tell Rob. A young, rail-thin man in suspenders walks onstage and begins thrumming a stand-up bass so curvaceous and perfectly bronzed it makes him look sickly. Another man old enough to be his grandfather tunes a Telecaster and pokes at his pedal board with the toe of his boot.

"Todd thinks you want to fuck him," Rob whispers. "You do, don't you?"

I don't want to fuck Todd. I just enjoy his company.

"Nobody's fucking anyone," I tell him, taking a big, searing drink.

The band noodles their way through "Rocky Top" and then something else like it. Todd takes me for a clumsy spin and Rob's head slowly begins to explode.

People start taking pictures and honestly, I'm asking for it. Todd slings his arm around me. I lean into him and feel my eyelids flutter. I *am* drunk.

Rob gets his compartments back. Even in a shit mood, he's a professional with a job to do. I'm hustled out the door wordlessly and lifted into the car.

"He was groping you," Rob says as Broadway glows behind us. His voice is filled more with hurt than outrage. "He definitely wanted to fuck you."

Todd wasn't groping me, but I let Rob spin and spin until he drops me off. I'm not being nice.

• • •

The next day Rob picks me up looking wounded. I look wounded too. My face is swollen and puffy, with cloudlike cheeks and a small red mouth made redder by the Gatorade I chugged for breakfast. I haven't been this hungover since college. I owe Rob an apology.

"I'm sorry about last night," I tell him, as he idles by the curb. It's too sunny out. Neither of us are in any mood for sunshine.

"It's fine," he says flatly. "I'm quitting anyway. I'm not going to sit here and watch you screw other guys."

For a moment, it really does seem like a sensible choice. But I'm struck by how much I don't want him to quit. And I don't like losing. And I *like* him.

"It was just a bad night," I reason.

"Who do you want to be—the 'party mayor'?" Rob makes air quotes and talks with a stupid voice, something he does often. "Or do you want to be taken seriously?"

We sit in silence. We've been working together almost a full year and sleeping together half that time.

"We should stop," I say.

"We should," he agrees.

We could stop anytime through fall and winter, we certainly intend to, but we don't.

• • •

It's February 10 and I'm on the plane with the chief of police, his media liaison, Rob, and several other officers. We are flying back from Ohio, where we were attending the funeral of a fallen MNPD officer, when I see everyone look down at their phones.

"Ma'am, there's been an incident," the chief says. He sounds the way they all do when they have bad news. Grave and unshakable.

He describes in detail what has happened: a young Black man was shot running away from the police earlier in the afternoon in Cayce, a housing project on the east side of town. The man was armed, but he'd dropped his weapon. The chief clears his throat, waiting for me to fully absorb the information.

Another white cop shot another Black man. It sounds like more than a fucking incident to me.

All I can think about is a mother sitting in a curtained hospital room wondering if she'll ever see her son again. I remind myself to compartmentalize, do my job, do it well, and leave every part of me that is not mayor at home.

Sean meets me at police headquarters to watch the video of the shooting.

"What can we do?" I ask Sean.

"Right now?" he replies, thinking for a moment. "Nothing. Release a statement of condolence maybe? That's really all you can do."

"Shit," I say to myself.

"Shit," he says to himself.

Together, we sit down to draft something.

"I appreciate that the MNPD has been forthcoming in quickly releasing information about the shooting. There will be a full and thorough investigation of all the facts in this case before any final judgments are rendered. My thoughts and prayers are with the friends and family of Mr. Clemmons and all those grieving his loss."

I have never wanted to be the kind of leader who sends her "thoughts and prayers" and nothing fucking else.

Over the next month, "let the police do their job," "let the Tennessee Bureau of Investigation do their job," and "let the DA do his job" are the lines we take. It feels entirely insufficient, but I simply don't have a lot of power. I can marshal parades and issue an executive order declaring it Nashville Predators Pride Day, but I can't walk onto a crime scene like Mariska Hargitay and interfere with an ongoing investigation. I can sack the police chief, but he's a good police chief and we need him right now. I focus on the good I can do. I talk to the family of the victim, who wants nothing to do with me; the NAACP; and other community leaders. We finally launch Opportunity NOW, the paid internship program inspired by the person I hoped Max would become, but who he decidedly is not. We celebrate the Cherry Blossom Festival and Record Store Day. The city keeps moving. Whether or not it should, I don't know.

The police department and the Tennessee Bureau of Investigation argue with each other about what happened on February 10, but by the end of spring, in spite of themselves, they manage to cobble together a report. The DA rules that the officer acted in self-defense. After reviewing the DA's decision, I offer him my support. The evidence to prove there were other motivations or gross negligence simply doesn't exist. The evidence that systemic change is urgently needed is everywhere.

"You can't worry about that police stuff," a council member says to me the afternoon the decision comes through. "It isn't even your job."

But isn't it exactly my job? To give a shit?

I address the city in a press conference, urging the citizens to stay calm, calling for change, and promising that the government will work to restore trust. They don't believe me. And I don't blame them.

• • •

Bruce and I go out west for Max's graduation, so I'm not in town on the evening of May 12. Black Lives Matter protesters arrive outside my home dressed in dark clothing, carrying signs and a black coffin. I support Black Lives Matter. I have shouted, "No justice, no peace." If it were another city, another life, I'd be shouting it along with them, calling for change and better leadership. I watch the demonstration on the news, at a distance like everyone else.

"You Did This"
"Stop Letting the Police Get Away with Killing Black People"
"Body Cameras NOW"

I read every single sign they leave leaned up against the fence. They have a right to do this. They should be doing this. I don't make all the decisions, but I do shoulder the fallout. That's my job.

The office scrambles around trying to put together the right statement, weighing the pros and cons of every phrase, analyzing the implications of a comma or a period, before abandoning it altogether. There are no words. There is no justice, no peace.

Two long, somber days later, we watch Max walk across the stage in a silly black cap and gown. For the first time in a long time, I wonder if I'm making him proud, if I'm the person he hoped I would be. And I can't be sure.

Max is good. He's always been good. Maybe he won't get an MBA or head up a nonprofit. Maybe he'll be a DJ who lives with his parents. The world needs DJs.

I smile as they call his name.

"Max H Barry."

I'm glad we never made him a Maxwell or a Maximilian. He's a Max.

Bruce cheers. My mother takes pictures with her cell phone camera, which she's not entirely sure how to use. My dad and his partner, Sig, are with us. Mom and Dad refrain from bickering for now, for the sake of Max, and me probably. Sig mouths "sorry" at me while my dad keeps jumping up and trying to get a glimpse of Max. They've been together since I was about twenty.

It's hard not to be consumed with awe when I see my dad, since I am now also a philanderer. I remember the good-looking men who came in and out of his life. The friend at college who helped him paint house numbers on the street to make extra money, all those friends of the family. He worked long and late hours, just like me. I could never imagine I'd turn out be just like him. He made my mother miserable.

I look over at Bruce. He's clapping. Max just grabbed the little tube of paper, which looks miniature in his hand. If Bruce is miserable, it's impossible to tell. If he's elated, it's impossible to tell. I clap along with him.

"We did it," Max jokes, clambering down from the stage and giving us all one of his giant hugs. He's sweating and he smells funny. Chemicals from the robe, I guess.

"Thank you for coming all the way out here," he says with a smile and genuinely means it. He loves his grandparents.

"Oh, honey! We are so proud of you!" my mom exclaims, weepy eyed. She takes Max's arm. The two of them and Sig wander off to discuss the height of Mount Rainier. Bruce goes off by himself, looking somewhere between miserable and elated.

"Megan," my dad says seriously. As seriously, at least, as a man wearing knee-high socks and a black-and-white fedora can do anything. "You know Max is high, right?"

Another Living Thing

It's a Saturday in July. The weather is cooler than it should be. There's nothing on my schedule and I'm home, a rarity. The sun is shining, and I'm in a blissful haze that feels something like contentment. My mind fills with trivial questions that require no answers. *Did I leave the back door open? Where did I leave my coffee? Is Hank on the front porch or under the kitchen table?* Moments later, he barks at passersby on their way to the local breakfast joint, answering the question for me. Should I text Max? Of course I should. I type at 10:51 AM:

> Are you up?

A harmless message. Not the kind of thing I expect to read over and over or save on each subsequent phone I'll ever own. I look at the time stamp, 10:51 AM, noting it with no inkling that it would mark the beginning of the worst day of my life. I sit in the sun and wait.

I text Max again at 12:11 PM:

> Do you have time to talk or are you headed to work?

No response.

I text again at 12:27 PM:

> Call me.

And he does.

Max and I talk. It's not memorable; it's like a thousand other conversations we've had. My favorite talks are the ones where we have nothing really important to say. I wander in and out of the house. I can let my mind drift. I can remember when his feet were small, sweet smelling, and shaped like Sister Schubert's dinner rolls. I listen less to his words and more to the low, rumbly timbre of his voice, which I swear deepened overnight at fifteen. He hangs up accidently, and we text again.

He texts at 1:18 PM:

> You almost said something and then I hung up my bad.

I reply at 1:21 PM:

> Just that I love you! Have a great day.

He responds at 1:22 PM:

> I love you too.

Hank gives chase to some unsuspecting squirrels, and I stick my head outside to call him back. He comes around the house, limping. *Damn it. Something's not quite right.*

Hank is Max's dog, the dog he's had since he was a child. Hank slept next to Max the night he hit his first home run in Little League and the night before we sent him off to rehab. Hank still sleeps in Max's room, stretching out on Max's comforter, expectant that his boy will come home any minute. Bruce and I watch Hank closely; he's hobbling slightly but not seemingly distressed. We aren't worried.

Bruce and I decide to have a night out. It'll be just the two of us, no security detail, at a local restaurant where we know the chef. The perfect afternoon has surrendered into a perfect rosy dusk, and we just want to sit at the bar, have a cocktail and good food, and connect like we used to, before every public outing became more like a campaign event, with me listening patiently to constituents and obliging by taking countless selfies, and Bruce receding into the background, annoyed. This is us trying. And I'm glad that we are.

Before we leave, I call Max to tell him about Hank's leg. I also give him grief about his motivation level, getting his act together, and smoking too much weed. He's chosen his Colorado path, which I'm trying and failing to respect. He's irritated but used to me by now.

"Quit busting his chops," Bruce says, after I hang up. But he says this fondly, smiling.

Max and I text throughout the evening. He writes at 7:08 PM:

> Really sucks you don't trust me and I've been doing Smazing with that shit for over a year. But I do love you and hope you trust me.

I respond at 7:09 PM:

> I DO trust you. And I do love you.

He texts back at 7:22 PM:

> That's all that matters. I value that so much Mainly because you'll love me no matter what. Trust is fantastic 🖤.

And then, his last one:

> All good Love you!!

I reply at 7:22 PM:

> Love you too.

Bruce and I go to dinner. I promise to politely ask anyone interrupting us to call me at my office on Monday and to limit picture taking. I promise to silence my phone and to focus my attention on my husband. And I do. We laugh. We're connecting. We're enjoying each other. We end our evening at home after a little too much to drink, and then we decide to have a little too much more.

Bruce pours us a nightcap and we sit out on the porch under the few but mighty stars. He plays DJ, curating the soundtrack of our life—Bruce Cockburn, Jackson Browne, John Prine, and Bonnie Raitt. There's an ease to us, for the first time in a long time. I begin to wonder how we'd fallen so out of touch when everything we'd loved in each other was here, outside the front door on a concrete slab with aggressive mosquitoes and a burnt-out porch light. In this moment, I'm in love. *We* are in love. He smokes a cigarette and tells me a story I haven't heard before. I throw my head back and laugh, feeling the respite of his eyes on me, of still being the one he wants and still being able to conjure "Meggie." Maybe all we needed to fix things was the proper ratio of good weather, vodka, music, and tree frogs. He grins at me and I'm heartsore. I know where I'm supposed to be. *How the hell did I let things with Rob get so out of control?*

Before we head upstairs for bed, around 10 PM, I switch my phone back on and see that I've missed a call from Max.

> 9:15 PM Missed call

I text him back at 9:55 PM:

> Saw I missed a call from you. Do you need me to call?

No response.

This is what I know about Max's evening. He is hanging out with friends on the back deck of a suburban house where one of his friends is housesitting. The guys are hungry and want something to eat. Max tells them to go without him. He's going to hang out. They can just bring him back some food.

I imagine him stretched out in a chair, tipping it back, taking a drag on a cigarette, and looking up at the twilight sky. I imagine him thinking about Hank and me and his dad and closing his eyes and being grateful for the moment. Perhaps this is when the drugs kick in, a lethal combination of Xanax, methadone, hydromorphone, and cocaine. Perhaps he knows something is wrong and he thinks of the one person who can help him. And he calls me. And my phone is on silent. And I miss his call.

His friends are gone forty minutes. By the time they get back, Max is having a seizure. He is overdosing, but these are twenty-something-year-old boys, and they don't know what to do. They throw water on him and hope it helps. Finally, one of them has the wherewithal to pick up the phone and dial 911. The paramedics are there by 9:58. They give him two doses of Narcan, but it doesn't help. He is gone by 10:30.

He is dying as I am texting him.

Bruce and I go to bed happy. At 2:00 AM, there's a knock on our door. I look at my phone. I've missed several calls. Bruce shoots up and out of bed with his Einstein hair, straight from his back to his feet. He's in a T-shirt with a giant moose emblazoned on the front and boxers. I'm in the light-blue floral pajamas I've worn since I was pregnant with Max. They lost their elasticity years ago, and I have to grab them by the waist so they don't fall as we head downstairs.

Through the window, I see Rob with his hands in his pockets and wish I looked a little less like the wallpaper in the women's powder room at the country club. There's another cop in uniform behind him.

Shit. There must have been a police shooting, I think.

I take a shallow sip of breath and prepare myself. I'll need to say something and get dressed. I'll need to drink water and take some ibuprofen. I can put my makeup on in the car and make Rob stop for a Diet Coke at the Circle K.

Bruce looks at me with the matte, bloodshot eyes of someone who's also going to have to reschedule their hangover for another time. I look back at him with as much sympathy as I can. I'm hungover too.

I open the door and Rob pushes his way through. He looks nice. He's taken the time to shower and he's wearing a suit. He is clearly dressed for whatever is going to come next, whatever tragedy we are going to have to deal with together, and I run my hands through my hair. I don't think I'll have time to wash it.

It takes twelve steps to walk from our front door to our kitchen island. You pass the living room on the left and the stairs leading to the second floor on the right. By the sixth step, you are passing the old dining room, and two more steps brings you into the open-plan kitchen / family room combo. Four more steps and you can run your hand down the length of the black counter as you walk to the end of the island.

I'm six steps in before Rob says, "I'm so sorry, ma'am. Max is gone."

I don't hear him. I don't focus. They aren't real words. I'm still trying to figure out what dress to put on. *Can I get away with platform sandals? When was the last time I had a pedicure? Do I need to go ahead and wear my lightweight black boots—that's probably best for a somber occasion.*

Two more steps. I reach the edge of the counter and stop, recalling the last ten seconds.

"What did you say?"

"I'm so sorry, ma'am. Max is gone," he repeats, this time a little softer.

I turn to look him in the eye. To stare down his cruel joke. To make him flinch and tell me what, exactly, he is doing at my house, with me and my husband, in the middle of the night.

"What did you say?" I ask again. Something about Max? Not our Max.

Four more steps and I've reached the end of the counter. I look at Bruce. Rob swallows and fixes his eyes on my husband, readying himself to tell the man whose wife he's been sleeping with that his only son overdosed on a lounge chair in some place called Littleton, Colorado.

"I'm so sorry, Mr. Barry. Max is dead."

My husband and my lover stare at each other in a tender silence, in the kitchen where only days ago Rob had put his hands around my waist and pulled me into him, where years and years ago Bruce had done the same. Bruce's jaw stiffens. Rob looks down and clasps his hands together. Rob clears his throat. Bruce sighs. In a collection of shocked, wordless seconds, they exchange condolences through the thought transference that men seem to adopt in moments like these.

"I'm so sorry," Rob says, aloud. And I think he really is, for everything.

I am the only one who becomes an animal, who is totally undone and made wild by shock at new grief. I tear past them both, stumbling up the stairs and into our bedroom. I search for my phone so I can call Max and find out what the hell is going on. I need pants and a shirt and a bra and I need to brush my teeth. I collapse on the floor of our closet, unsure where reality begins and ends, knowing only to put socks on my feet and scream. Bruce stays downstairs with Rob. I wail. I sob. I know it's true. And no one comes.

• • •

I don't sleep at all through the last hours of night. I'm wide awake and horribly, painfully thunderstruck. Max is gone. The world has ended. But the breakfast place opens, the Sunday morning bells ring out from the campanile, and light climbs higher and fills the sky. Turrets of grill smoke come up over the fence from a few houses down, and a homeless cat crosses the road, tail standing straight in the air, in no rush to get anywhere.

My family arrives by midday and my friends arrive even sooner. Arrangements are being made. Statements are being written. Food is being prepared. Dog chow clatters into big, metal bowls. Groups come and go from the house like schools of fish, flowing in and out. There is everyone with a honey-baked ham and a casserole and booze, or there is no one at all. There is only too much love or too little. I'm not sure which is better. Bruce becomes incredibly useful, brewing coffee, walking the dogs, and opening the door when concerned faces appear in the long panes of glass. I just stare wide-eyed, trying to wrap my head around it. Bruce and I don't hug or cry. We don't talk about Max, mostly because we can't bear the shaky, brand-new language of "dids" and "wases" and "would haves." What would we even say?

How did we manage to miss how sick he was?

Why did I let him go to rehab in fucking Florida?

What do we wish we'd said to him?

What do we wish we hadn't?

How angry are we?

How broken?

Bruce makes phone calls and makes sure everyone has what they need to get by. He sets up in the house, hanging out on the back deck, and I cross my legs and position myself in an Adirondack chair on the front porch, where ten hours ago I was falling in love again with my husband.

Rob and Sheri drop by midday after church. I'm not expecting them. She comes carrying twelve rolls of Bounty paper towels with one arm and a whole world of Charmin with the other. Rob gives me a stiff professional hug. I smell his soap and let his breath brush the bottom of my ear, but only for a second. We've rehearsed this quiet moment of intimacy enough times at work that it's totally undetectable to the human eye.

"Oh, Megan! I'm so sorry. I just can't believe it," Sheri whispers.

She drops everything the second she summits the steps to embrace me, which I allow, because we really do need toilet paper. She continues inside with her sundries, ready to fix it all, which I also allow. Rob and I are alone.

"Why are you here? Why did you bring her here?" I whisper-yell at him when his devastated wife is a safe distance away.

"She just wants to help." He pinches the bridge of his nose between two fingers and shakes his head. "I don't know. I don't know why. I'm sorry."

I spot Sheri and her floral dress in the living room headed toward Bruce. She gives him a long and tight squeeze. Bruce stands in a state of stiff astonishment and graciously lets it happen.

● ● ●

Max's visitation is Monday at the Blair School of Music on Vanderbilt's campus, not too far from where Bruce teaches. I wear a black dress and blazer, what Max used to call my "mayor clothes." We decide not to wait for the body, *his* body, to arrive from Colorado. The longer we wait, the more the press will write about him. The longer we wait, the more the story will mutate into something worse; the more it will spin, spin, spin; and the more opportunities the media will have to play the 911 call of his last few minutes. The local Nashville TV stations have a copy, and Max's second-grade teacher, his basketball coach, and strangers across Nashville hear Max take his last breath and his friends screaming.

"Don't listen to it," Sean warns me. I don't.

I won't let it become a spectacle. Max wouldn't want that. He lost a battle he couldn't even admit to fighting, not even to me, his own mother. He wasn't looking for coverage.

Panicky gray squirrels with trash in their mouths (Hank's favorite) dart across the insanely green collegiate lawn as Bruce and I walk toward the building. I watch them zip around, frenetic and paranoid, presumably wracking their little brains to remember where they stowed all those nuts. A distance away, mourners snake in a great big line around the great glass building. I don't recognize a single person. A half-dozen news trucks are parked haphazardly on the roadside, guarded by derelict, half-smashed traffic cones that quite obviously have not done their job well in the past.

"Jesus," I breathe, wincing at the people in their black clothes around the block, remembering that they're here for our son.

I turn my attention again to the squirrels, who keep searching and searching, scurrying and jolting, not knowing what it is to lose someone, only what it is to lose four acorns in a park. Bruce is watching them too. Beyond logistics, he and I have hardly spoken.

"Remember when Hank actually caught one?" I say to Bruce, too anesthetized to realize I'm talking at all.

"Yep," he says, walking ahead and remembering quietly along with me.

Max was home alone. After years of study and countless hours of pursuit, Hank mortally wounded one of the tiny, twitchy squirrels from the walnut tree out back. It was 80 percent dead by the time Hank relinquished it to him. There was blood all over his snout, an unsettling picture of a childhood dog for anyone. The squirrel lay on a dishrag looking up at Max with an empty black eye, flanks rising and falling, rising and falling, with its final few breaths of life. Max didn't want it to suffer; he never wanted anything or anyone to suffer. He placed it in the sun and Googled "humane ways to kill squirrels." After evaluating his options, he scooped it up in a Kroger bag, tied it to the back of his muffler, and started the car. The bag filled up with carbon monoxide. The squirrel died quickly and mercifully. I'd always wished I'd been there with him, not because he wasn't brave enough, but more because he was.

When we finally got home, Max was shaken and pale. He told me that the internet had first suggested he bludgeon the squirrel to death with a shovel. The thought of pounding it to death twisted his beautiful, gentle face into sadness.

"I couldn't do that, Momma. I could never hurt another living thing."

He had taken his glasses off and rubbed his eyes. Max never, ever wanted to cause pain, no matter how much of it he lived with himself.

I wish I'd known he was in trouble, but Max was good at keeping secrets. His suffering never made him callous or cruel. It never stole the beauty of a clear day or dulled the magic of cool water, thick forest, or big sky. He loved Walt Whitman and Tupac Shakur and all the sweet, simple shapes that peace takes in the world—good dogs, back decks, laughter, the state of Colorado. I thought he was happy and healthy and free.

Give him peace, I pray quietly to myself.

My boots hit the asphalt and shock me back into reality. Bruce places a hand on my back, and we walk past the crowd and smile.

"Thank you for coming. Thank you for coming. Thank you for coming."

Pushing open an impossibly heavy door to an impossibly heavy room, we get ready to say goodbye.

Give us peace, I pray again and again.

Funeral Underwear

We have to figure out a way to bring Max's body back to Nashville. Back to the place where he started his life, back to his home. Max is our son. Max *was* our son. How do I even begin to use the past tense?

My friend Anna, who recently lost her nephew to cancer, tells me, "Call the undertaker. He can help."

"Call the undertaker. He can help," is jarring advice to receive no matter how close you are to accepting your reality. I receive it with gratitude, thinking briefly about how jarring it must be to have lived through her loss and to know to suggest it.

I pick up the phone and dial Wilbur's number, and he greets me with a voice that is filled with all the warmth and compassion and Southern love that comes from being in the business of burying people. I am grateful.

"Wilbur, I need your help," I stammer into the receiver. "We need to bring Max home."

Wilbur tells me of his sorrow at my loss and offers to help. Any way he can.

"Mayor . . ." he begins, using my title.

"Call me Megan, please call me Megan," I say. Megan was Max's mom.

"I'm going to do my best to get things sorted for you today," he continues, "but I'm just gonna tell you up front, I don't deal with big funeral."

I am unfamiliar with "big funeral."

He goes on to explain, "Now, I don't deal with all those corporate businesses, you know, the funeral chains. We, in the business, call 'em 'big funeral,' and I'm going to have to find me an in-dee-pendent operator who will go and get Max from the morgue, and that may just be tough at this hour."

It's nearly 4 PM. Since death isn't a nine-to five gig, I figured the morgue wouldn't be either. Wilbur assures me he can make this happen, but he'll need time. I thank him.

"And one more thing," he cautions. "We gotta be careful. Most of these in-dee-pendent operators also like to do some things on the side, you know, like taxidermy, and they do it out of their ghee-rahges, and I don't want Max coming back to you with a stuffed squirrel sewed to his forehead."

On this point, Wilbur and I agree. Neither of us wants a dead animal sewn to my dead child.

He tells me he'll get back to me in a while when he has something to report. I leave Max's transport back to Nashville in his capable hands.

While I lose myself in this small errand of death, Bruce handles the big stuff. I don't want to see anyone. I don't want to write a statement for the public or pretend at courage. I want to mourn. I want to be shell-shocked in my kitchen. I want to forget to eat and have my sisters do my laundry. Mostly, I want Bruce, but Bruce is suddenly cyclonic. He's frenetic and focused in a way I haven't seen him since the campaign. Bruce is all checklists and research and touching base with various relatives and friends. Bruce is walking the dogs four times a day and doing dishes and providing updates to anyone who might need them, though there aren't many updates in a situation this final. He asks how I'm doing and makes me coffee (with Truvia) and hugs me, but in a way that makes me feel as though I'm just part of the mania. I let him spin around me, which, dizzyingly, he does. The body is mine; everything else is his.

Wilbur calls back to let me know that Max has been collected from the morgue and is being prepared to be shipped home. Bodies have to be embalmed before they can cross state lines, so Wilbur informs me that it will take more time, more steps, before Max will be back where he belongs. Paperwork needs to be completed. Boxes checked.

The questions now are:

Will we bury him?

What are our plans for him when he returns?

I picture Max resting under an elm in the cemetery off Fourth, somewhere peaceful and green, far away from the general and his eagle. I wonder if I could give my plot to him since I don't need it . . . yet. This is one of the more awful things I have wondered about.

Wilbur's "non-big funeral" funeral home calls me to ask how I want Max to look. They're getting ready to cut his long, beautiful hair, and to shave his scruffy beard, something I begged him to do a thousand times. But I want Max to look like Max. The idea of him looking like anything other than a twenty-two-year-old aspiring DJ is suddenly blasphemous.

"Don't touch him," I say. "Just send him back to me. Just send him back to Nashville. Just send him home."

And that's what they do.

Bodies that are embalmed come home on planes. In the belly of a Southwest flight from Denver. In a cardboard box that says "Fragile," and "This End Up." Seriously. As cargo.

Wilbur tells me that we can meet Max after they off-load him at the airport and that he will then take Max via hearse to the funeral home.

And he tells me, "Megan, I'm gonna need some clothes. Now, you know Max is gonna come back in that cardboard box and he isn't gonna have any clothes with him, so we're going to need to have some. And we have a policy—everyone we deal with has to get buried in underwear. It's just how we do things. So, you'll need to bring that along with his clothes."

Jesus.

Max has been at college for the last four years and everything he owns, including his underwear, is in Colorado. Not in Nashville. I tell Wilbur we'll see him there. With underwear.

When I get off the phone, I pad around the house looking for Bruce. I find him at his computer looking thinner and older than he did hours ago.

"Hey," I tell him, "We need to get Max underwear."

"He doesn't have any?" Bruce asks in a monotone.

"He doesn't," I say back.

Even if he did, I couldn't bear the idea of going into his room. Not yet.

"I'm going to go get him something to wear," I tell him.

I'm thinking and hoping in this moment that Bruce will get up. He will get the car keys. He will buy Max's funeral underwear with me if for no other reason than I won't have to make small talk with a check-out girl and remind her nicely that I would not like a Target rewards card because my son is dead. I don't give a shit about the 10 percent off my purchase.

Bruce doesn't even look at me.

My sisters step in and we go to the sporting goods store and pick out what was always Max's uniform—a white T-shirt, Nike athletic shorts, and a baseball cap (which he always wore backwards). When I take my purchases to the counter, the young man hugs me and says, "These are on us, these are for Max." We stop at Target for underwear, which only comes in packs of three. I have extra.

We meet Max at the freight part of the Nashville airport. Music is blasting through the speakers. At first, I think it's "Werewolves of London," but the lyrics aren't right. It's Kid Rock singing a song about getting shit-housed on whiskey, being young and stupid where it's summer forever and there are no consequences. But there are always consequences and he's not a fucking "kid."

I watch the conveyor belt gently rock a long brown cardboard box as it rumbles up into Wilbur's brand-new hearse. My baby is home.

Wilbur is exactly what I pictured, medium build and full of light. He leads us on a caravan to the funeral home in his sedan, which is followed by the hearse, then me, then my sisters. Bruce is still at home. He had simply said, "I can't," when I'd asked if he wanted to come to the airport.

With our flashers on, we slowly roll down Murfreesboro Pike to Antioch Pike, to Blue Hole Road, to Pettus Road, to Old Hickory Boulevard, to Nolensville Road. When we arrive at the chapel, a couple of men in suits lift Max's box into the building. The next time I see my son, he'll be in a coffin.

My sisters stay with Max at the funeral home, and I go and pick up Bruce to take him to see our son. By the time we're back, Wilbur has prepared a private viewing room and Max is waiting for us. My sisters, Heather, Kristin, and Molly, are standing outside. I can't bear to go in and see him if he looks different. If there is indeed a squirrel sewed to his head. My sisters reassure me.

"He looks just like Max," they say.

And he does—long, brown hair, finely tapered fingers, a baseball hat on backwards with the brim tucked under. His hands are laid out perfectly folded in front. The way dead people are displayed. Max is dead. But otherwise, he looks just fine.

. . .

I go back to work, and mercifully, it takes me far away from Nashville and today and right now. People in other places want to learn from me. I'm still the woman mayor, the one who is throwing open the doors to make Nashville a warm and welcoming place, the bringer of hope to little girls. I go to San Francisco and Washington, DC, to attend meetings, summits, and events while the team holds down the fort in Nashville through the fall. They think it will be good for me to get away, and it is. Rob is with me. He holds me because Bruce can't or won't or doesn't know how, and I return the favor. He becomes my alternate reality, the space where I am not the mother of a dead child.

My family organizes a memorial service for Max in Kansas City on the back porch of my cousin's home. The city sends Rob as my detail, and Bruce stays behind. My mother weeps and we hug each other. She talks in whispers, a mixture of pride and sorrow. I steal away from her, from everything, when I can, but she watches across the room with owl eyes taking inventory of glances, gestures, and the precise length of time Rob's fingers rest on my elbow, how low his hand rests on my back.

When the mourners begin to clear and the sun sets low over the flatness of the city, she "borrows" me from Rob and wraps me in her arms. She pulls me in close, squeezing my ribs into hers, and whispers, "Megan, you are so stupid. You are going to lose everything."

I want to tell her that I already have.

Deny, Deny, Deny

Rob and I are in Paris at a hotel bar. It's October. Balanced on the starched white arms of waiters, large bowls of *moules et frites* pass by us, steaming, smelling like garlic and the ocean. I'm numb, which is making it hard to enjoy the exaggerated Frenchness around me: accordion music, wall sconces that look like streetlights, the same mass-produced *Tournée du Chat Noir* poster that everyone puts in their first grown-up kitchen, even in Nashville, even in Tacoma. I miss Max so much it takes my breath away.

Rob's leg is touching mine, comfortably. He orders me another martini, communicating to the waiter across the room with only his fingers. Somehow, he manages to do this in a way that feels charming and not obnoxious. The waiter practically winks back at him, as though to say (in as French a way as possible), "I got you, bro. I always got you." Rob smiles at me and he's exactly what I need him to be, doting, handsy, swept away. Someone who can help me remember who I was and forget who I am. My gaze floats across the room into a mirrored wall, backlit and covered halfway in bottles of Aperol, Chartreuse, crème de cassis, and, for good measure, Puff Daddy's vodka. I see Max. My boy. There he is above the squat brown bottle of Grand Marnier, in my eyes, my lips, the bow of my chin. I look away.

Several of my staff members wander over. "We're headed back to the hotel," one says. "We start at eight tomorrow." They're with me on this trip and they all look exhausted.

They all rub their eyes like sleepy babies, making a fruitless attempt to shake off the jet lag. We're traveling with Bloomberg Philanthropies for CityLab, an international summit dedicated to making the world's greatest cities greater by sharing ideas and talking about the future. My staff has been excited about this for months. It's Mayorfest 2017. I have never seen so many white-toothed, white-haired, white men in one place in my life.

As someone is talking about the schedule for tomorrow, Rob tucks a piece of hair behind my ear. A wave of panic crests and falls over me. My coworkers are all only a few feet away. *Do they know? Does everyone know?*

But they don't notice. They don't suspect a thing. Rob could pick me up, mount me over the bar, and make love to me singing "La Vie en rose" and no one would believe we were having an affair. Their trust in me is deep. Deep enough to make us reckless—inside jokes whispered into each other's ears, hands lingering, smiles that are both too frequent and too familiar. My colleagues aren't taking inventory. Yet. But they will.

"See you then," I say to them all. "Sleep well."

One of them looks at me with concern for a second, maybe to ask if I'm okay getting up to my room and then decides against it. Rob is here. There's no reason to worry.

They leave and Rob moves in closer. He murmurs, "I love being here with you."

His words are simple. His breath is salty and bathwater warm.

We walk to the elevator, and before the doors are fully closed, Rob cradles the back of my head and kisses me.

• • •

Through the fall, there's too much Max in Nashville and too much Bruce, so I make my schedule exactly what I need it to be: brutal and punishing. I say yes to everything. I don't even bother inviting Bruce anymore. While the pace of life has lulled me into an ultra-productive, type A stupor, Bruce is lost in time. He plods around the house, going to work and coming home and eating, going to work and coming home and reading, going to work and coming home and sitting with the dogs, as though Max is still here. He doesn't want to talk about it, acknowledge it, or look it or me in the eye. He outright refuses. I need more, so I talk to CNN and NPR and NBC. I speak at events, rattling off statistics about the opioid crisis and promising change. Largely, I'm regarded as heroic in this arena, someone willing to have hard conversations, someone determined to make a difference. And I am determined. I'm also determined to get my transportation plan approved, to win a second term, and to live my life while I still have it. If not with Bruce, then maybe with someone who is still calling me "nice" and "great" and "pretty" and "smart." Someone who helps me forget the things I've lost so that I can keep getting up every day.

According to Nashville, I'm soldiering on. Sean is good at his job and I'm good at mine, and together, we've spun this whole thing into gold. Politics is probably more like alchemy than it should be. My approval rating is astronomical. I'm cruising toward a second term. Only the people closest to me know the way things really are. I'm not talking to my husband. I'm drowning in grief. I am not okay.

• • •

It's mid-November. Bruce and I have received thousands of letters, cards, emails, gifts, and stories of loss since Max died, but there is one correspondent who is different. Twice a week, since August, we've received a card in the mail from an Ohio address neither Bruce nor I know in a town we've never heard of.

Standing on the front porch, held generously in a beam of late-afternoon sun, I open the latest card, a sky-blue envelope, shut tightly. The smell of adhesive and thick, fancy paper hits me in the nose as I slide the card out. It's expensive and store-bought, with embossed lettering and white flowers on the front offering condolences for loss. I open it. Two words are handwritten at the bottom, the same two words as always: "Lovingly, Debby."

I'm crying.

I don't know you.

Who are you?

Why are you doing this?

Did you lose someone?

Do you have dementia?

I want her to stop. The condolences are over now. I've got shit to do. I shove the card into my purse and open the door, letting my body fall onto the couch with Hank and Boris.

I text Bruce:

> It's a Debby day.

The only thing we communicate about other than Hank and Boris these days is the Debby cards.

He replies:

> Should we send her something back? A lock of your hair?

I laugh out loud. My staff, rightly, is worried we're in *Single White Female* territory, but I think we're just dealing with a good Christian lady. He ventures:

> A signed headshot?

I laugh again. Max would laugh too. I picture him, moon-shaped circles under his eyes, messy hair roofed by a backwards ballcap, lips curled into a perfect grin.

Three days later, another letter arrives, signed "Lovingly, Debby." Two days after that, another.

• • •

It's just after New Year's and I'm in the French Quarter with eight of my girlfriends. This is not a work trip. We're catching up, and eating and drinking our way down Bourbon Street, not knowing where one bar ends and another begins. I love my girlfriends, and they may suspect things with Bruce aren't great, but none of them know about Rob and I don't intend on telling them.

Balconies draped in greenery, leftover Christmas lights, and omnipresent clusters of shimmering purple beads rise up around us, and the air is still spiced with evergreen. In the space between Santa Claus and Mardi Gras, the city is quiet, smelling more like roux than Axe body spray. I like it here. I always have.

We pour out of Lafitte's Blacksmith Shop and onto the cobblestones. Celia Mae wants to get a tarot reading done. Celia Mae is a kick-ass attorney with a slightly above average interest in the occult.

She pulls out her phone and begins Yelp-ing her way to a reputable fortune teller, if such a thing exists.

"It's silly, but this stuff does fascinate me," I shrug. I'm curious.

"We're not far from Madame Marie Laveau's House of Voodoo," she reports, taking a long sip of her freshly procured Pat O'Brien's hurricane. "I'll go online, and we can sign up for an appointment on the way."

After a minute, she says, "Shoot. It'll be hours before there's a slot. Do you want to wait that long?"

"Nope," I respond. "Do you?"

"No. I'm hungry. Let's find some food."

The future can wait.

We continue down Bourbon, and at the corner of St. Ann, there's a young woman with a small card table and a deck of tarot cards. She's thin and pale, with a leather vest and hair that was bleached yellow some time ago. A thick brunette stripe runs down the middle of her head. She looks up at us.

"Hey! She can be our substitute," I say.

Celia Mae looks disappointed. Apparently, Madame Laveau takes Visa and gives you tea. This fortune teller is fresh out of velvet robes and oolong. She does have a stick of Nag Champa burning, but she looks more like Christina Aguilera than the all-knowing Zoltar.

"I'm doing it," I say and walk toward my fate and the three-legged dog at her feet.

"Hi! Can you do a reading for me?" I ask.

She nods, almost like she doesn't have the energy for words. She's tired looking and skeletal, but I ignore the track marks on her arms and decide that whatever she tells me I will embrace with enthusiasm. It's New Orleans, after all. She motions to a folding chair opposite her. I sit.

She lays out the cards neatly on her table. First, Justice, with a sword in her right hand, the double edges signifying consequences. Then, in quick succession, two sword cards, the Seven of Swords, and the Ten of Swords.

"They're coming for you," she says as she looks me in the eye. Her pupils are so small I can barely see them.

"February will be a horrible month. Prepare yourself for betrayal and deception and painful endings. By March, it will all be over."

The way she says "painful" causes an ache in my chest.

Fuck me.

I'm too stunned to ask any questions, so I just watch the worry lines appear between her brows. She stares imploringly into my eyes, as though to say, *Can't you see it too?*

Of course, I can.

A slight drizzle falls, at just enough of a volume to break our silence.

"It'll be fifty," she says. I hand her a crisp bill and walk away.

My girlfriends have wandered down the street and I catch up, trotting staccato along the slick cobblestones.

"What did she say?" Celia Mae asks. "Is 2018 going to be a great year for you, or what?"

"Or what," I say, rolling my eyes. "She's just a junkie. What does she know?"

I look back at the girl, who is counting bills and stuffing them into a zippered bag.

"I think she was high," I mutter.

* * *

Rob picks me up on Monday after my weekend away. The sky is a brilliant blue and all seems right with the world.

"God, I missed you," he says. I grab his hand, traveling the hills and valleys of his knuckles, tracing his blue, branchlike veins. I missed him too.

We pick up coffee from Fido, our normal routine, and drive to the cemetery, where the trees are black and naked and the grass is dead. Even now, in the starkness of January, I love it here.

We roll along the laneway and stop underneath what will look like a dogwood again by April.

I ask how his weekend was.

"Sheri thinks she's really onto me this time," he complains, shaking his head and laughing.

"No! I'm sorry," I say with sympathy, for him, not her.

She's sure Rob is sleeping around again, but so far, my name hasn't come up.

Mostly, Rob doesn't seem to mind being accused of philandering. I think a part of him enjoys it. Sheri sniffs around, panics, and cries; she lives caught in the agony of neither totally trusting him nor finding a concrete reason not to. He brings her to city events. She and I make polite conversation while he stands across the room mouthing "I love you" at me. When I excuse myself, he follows me to the bathroom where he can show me in a dark corner how hard he is. I don't like being a part of it. But I also can't stop.

Around 7:30 AM, when we're headed to the office, his phone rings.

"There she is again," he says with a sigh.

He doesn't take it and instead tucks his cell away.

As we drive down Second Avenue toward the courthouse, I tell him about New Orleans, and he tells me about dinner club, a book signing with his friend Bob, the farmers market, the gym.

"I'm jealous," I tell him. It makes him chuckle. "I'm jealous of your life."

I say it mostly to be nice, but it's true. I am jealous of his life. Because he gets to have one—a normal one with leg presses at the Y and dinner club, with an alive grown-up kid and an adoring spouse. For a moment,

I wonder what it's like in the alternate reality where we're together, going to church in the morning and watching the Titans game with friends in the afternoon, complimenting the surround sound, the jalapeño poppers, the well-behaved dog.

The drive takes thirteen minutes. We pull into the garage and get out, pausing outside the stairwell door for a kiss and a slap on the ass. Then, we walk upstairs to work.

Around 8 AM, in the middle of our staff meeting, Rob's phone rings again. And again. He excuses himself, something he never does. I watch him outside the door while Sean talks about my Twitter feed. Rob is pacing. His face is dumb and paper white. He looks weak.

My team filters out of the room and Rob rushes in.

"Sheri heard our conversation."

Rob never declined Sheri's call that morning. She listened to us talk for thirteen minutes and she swears she heard him say, "I love you."

"What now?" he asks, eyes wide and terror filled.

"Deny it," I say. "Deny, deny, deny."

• • •

The next morning somebody else picks me up in the Tahoe. Rob doesn't come in for several days, and when he does, he's disheveled. I know what's coming.

He walks into my office, shuts the door, and sits next to me on my too-expensive couch. His hand rests gently on my thigh, his long fingers unconsciously stroking my dress. I can feel his warmth through my clothes. He looks like hell.

"Sheri knows," he says and then looks away.

"How can she know? She might suspect, but she can't know unless you told her. You didn't tell her, did you? You swore to God you wouldn't tell her, but you told her, didn't you?"

"I thought it would make things better," he says with a shrug. "Calm her down, you know, so she would stop asking me about it. I think it'll work. I had breakfast with a friend of mine who cheats on his wife a lot, and he told me when his wife gets this crazy, he just gives her a little satisfaction in thinking she's kind of right."

Jesus Christ. He's got a fucking mentor now.

"I have no idea what that means. You either told her or you didn't. Which is it?" I ask.

I don't want to be angry with him. I want to be supportive and kind. I have yet to confess anything to Bruce. I have continued to downplay Sheri's phone calls and text messages to Bruce asking him to call her as Sheri just "being Rob's crazy wife." God, I'm doing exactly what Rob has done to her all these years, calling her crazy. She isn't crazy. She's right.

"I told her that, yes, you and I did have some physical contact."

He looks down at his hands, stands up, and moves to a chair. "I told her we've kissed."

"You told her that all we did was kiss and she believed you?" I'm incredulous.

What are we in, fifth grade here?

"Not exactly. She started asking me more questions, like had I ever touched your breasts, or put my hand up your skirt, had you ever touched me, had we ever had sex?"

"Jesus, and?"

"Well, I said yes." It's the first time I've ever seen him look ashamed.

I am no longer kind and supportive. I am actively freaking out.

"Rob! We are so fucked. You did what you said you would never do. You confessed! God, how could you be so stupid? How could you, after all these years of cheating with so many people, pick this time to be honest? You always said that if Sheri found out, she would crucify me and you. I'm guessing that hasn't changed, has it?"

"She wanted to know if I love you," he says.

"And?"

"I told her no, but I do. I do love you, Megan. She's promised she's not going to tell anyone and she's going to stop contacting Bruce. She's going to keep our secret. I just have to promise to end it with you. It's going to be okay. She's won't do anything. She won't tell anyone."

I look at the deep lines around his blue eyes, his thinning hair, his slumped shoulders. He is a shell of himself. I want to help him and to rub away some of the worry and tell him it's all going to be okay. But I don't.

"You've got to go back to your office. I've got meetings. I've got work to do. How long do you think we have before she tells someone?" I prod.

Rob shrugs his shoulders. "I don't think she'll tell."

I swing my door open and call for Patrick.

"Patrick, whatever I have tonight, can we find someone to cover it? I need to go home."

Vice President, Morals and Standards

Sorority Elections, Alpha Chi Omega, Baker University, 1984

Megan Mueller: 37 votes

Kathy S.: 15 votes

"Oh, Megan! Oh, *Megan!* Congratulations! Can you believe it?!"

Cindy, a lovely, pink-skinned blonde, calls out frantically to me from the porch of the Alpha Chi Omega house. Her hair is the color of buttered popcorn (a recent mishap with the drugstore bleach) and her hands are crossed on her chest like she's about to do a trust fall, something we actually had to do during rush week.

Last night, I was elected vice president for morals and standards for the Baker University chapter of Alpha Chi Omega, an organization I joined because my mother told me I had to live at a sorority house if I wanted any financial help with my second attempt at college. Last year, I was flunking out of the University of Kansas with a 1.0 GPA and took a job at the local bank. I spent six months counting bills and cashing checks, work so soul crushing I couldn't begin to think about doing this for the rest of my days. Not all of us can be Joan Jett, but we don't all need to be bank tellers either. I'm going to be an elementary school teacher instead, which Mom says will leave me just enough time in the summers to be a decent wife and mother.

I thank Cindy, climb the porch steps, and walk into her now-open arms. She hugs me, long and hard. We stick together in the late-summer heat. Cindy is a big hugger and she's also the president of the entire sorority.

"I'm so happy you're here," she says with a grin, her round cheeks rising up to make her eyes into two small moons. "We don't get many transfers. Having your experience will be such an asset here."

The University of Kansas is not the cultural salon she thinks it is, but what she doesn't know won't hurt her. She settles into a white patio chair and offers me the one beside it, which I take, bristling as the hot plastic sears the backs of my thighs.

I haven't been at this school long, but they chose *me*; *I* won. The fact that I share a sleeping porch room with seven other girls—the most in the house by a serious margin—may have helped, but still, I won. When I came here, I met people, I listened to them, and I came up with a few ideas, like reworking the process for missing chapter meetings and instituting a mediation process for sisters at war.

A group of girls walk out onto the porch saddled with sagging book bags. They say hello to us both. I like that they know who I am.

Cindy opens a bag of Corn Nuts and throws a palmful into her ruddy cheek. I consider a cigarette but remember that smoking is prohibited on the front porch of the house and must instead occur on the back patio or the sidewalk. Upholding the rules is my job now, which is funny given how recently and doggedly committed I was to breaking them.

"Cindy?" I ask.

She turns to me, still crunching.

"I've never really done anything like this before. I don't even know what the vice president for morals and standards is supposed to do," I confess.

"Well," she chirps, "nobody knows what they're doing at first. All you need to do is help out. Make sure that everyone is showing good character and living up to our Alpha Chi Omega code. Just be a role model, Megan. Be yourself."

I nod. "Sounds easy enough."

Dead Vice Presidents

I let myself in the side door. The house is still dark. Bruce isn't home yet. I reach for a bottle of Cab, pull the cork, and give myself a very generous pour. I let the pups out but keep the house dark. Just for a moment, I revel in the little quiet before I have to face what comes next. I open my computer, sloshing the syrup-thick wine in my mouth, and log into Facebook, where the unhinged express themselves most freely. I click on Sheri's page and see pictures of her and Rob, on family vacations and dancing at their daughter's wedding. She's happy in almost all of them, beautiful, beaming, and younger than me. Then, a new post appears. It says something about trust and being betrayed by the one you love.

Fuck.

I shut my laptop. I don't have much time at all. I need to fix this. Spin it. Make it make sense to Bruce, to me.

I know better, of course. I spent fifteen years using PowerPoint to teach executives how to keep their dicks in their pants. This kind of thing never ends well. People find out, people get hurt, people get divorced. Bruce and I probably should get divorced, but shit, it didn't need to be like this. Why didn't I just say something?

The conversations we should have had come at me all at once, and I feel suddenly small, or the room feels suddenly big. I could have told him I needed him. I could have asked him why he didn't want to touch me. I could have told him I missed him. But it's too late now.

Bruce comes in the front door, switching on the lights one by one as he goes. The dogs are at his heels. They've always preferred him.

"Meggie, are you home?" he calls. "I thought you had something tonight. I wasn't expecting to see you home so early. Are you sick? Why are you sitting here in the dark?"

He hasn't called me "Meggie" in a long time. My throat tightens.

"I thought I would come home, and we could spend some time together." I shrug, trying and failing to do so casually. "What I had tonight wasn't that important, and I just feel like I haven't seen you in weeks. That's okay, right? You don't have anything?"

"No, it's fine. I don't have anything going on, but I wasn't planning on you for dinner. I thought you'd get fed at your event. We just have leftovers, enough for one, but I'm sure we can cobble together something," he says.

He looks happier than normal, or maybe he has been happier lately and I haven't noticed. I'm not sure.

He dumps his backpack on the dining room table and eyes my glass of wine.

"Already cocktailing, are we? I'll join you in a minute. Let me just get out of my work clothes and I'll be right back."

He claps his hands together and turns to the stairs.

"Wait," I yell. "Bruce, can you just hold me for a second? I just need a hug. It's been a really long day. Just a hug. Please."

Obviously confused, Bruce comes over and stands in front of me. I wrap my arms around his midsection. He holds me for about as long as he can tolerate, a few moments, and then squirms out of my grasp.

"I'll grab a drink and you can tell me what's up," he says.

I top off my glass and wait for him to pour himself a couple of fingers of rye.

"By the way," he says, "I got another call from Sheri today. Should I be answering these? She's also texting me. I know you keep telling me she's a little nuts. Just tell me what you want me to do. I can keep ignoring her, but it feels rude. She's always been nice to us, and I do love those homemade chicken biscuits she sends over with Rob in the morning. They're fabulous."

I would say Bruce is suddenly righteous, but he spends several hours a week teaching ethics. Either way, this righteousness comes at a terrible time. Sheri does send biscuits now and then, but I never felt great about eating them.

"Yeah, I don't think there's going to be any more of those," I say under my breath.

"What?" He chuckles. "Did you say something? I'm sorry. I missed it. I don't usually say stuff like this, but you really don't look good. Are you feeling okay? What's going on?"

I rake a hand through my hair, and it snags on my fingers. I'm sweating, which means I'm probably close to crying.

"Nothing." I smile. "It's just work. It was kind of a stressful day. I don't really want to get into it. Just all that running-the-city stress. I'm going to pull something together for us to eat. You want breakfast for dinner? I'll make eggs. I think we have bacon somewhere."

I root around in the fridge and find something I make into an omelet and pour myself another glass of wine. I let the gentle buzz numb me, easing me into what I know I have to do. I have to tell him. I'm going to upend our lives again, throw a bolt out of nowhere, be the bringer of displacement and defeat and sadness. It's another death. Only this time, I could have stopped it.

I crack eggs into a ceramic mixing bowl and spoon out the flecks of shell with the back of a spoon.

"You want those leftovers or this, B? I can make enough for both of us. Whatever works," I say. "And I'm probably not long for this world after I eat. I just want to crawl in bed and go to sleep."

I whisk the eggs into a sunny-colored goo, feeling sheepish and cowardly. I watch him decide under the kitchen lights, looking more handsome, more "mine," than I want him to.

"I'm in," he says with a nod. "I'll have what you're cooking, and then you should really go to bed. Don't stay up. We'll just eat, and I can close things up down here. You really look like you need a good night's sleep."

I cook the eggs. We eat dinner and tune in to catch Final Jeopardy!

"The Theater" is the category.

"'The Theater!'" Bruce scoffs. "Well, nobody wants that!"

Packing a lump of egg in his cheek, he's peeved. And he's right. Nobody ever wants "The Theater." The "The Theater" people are busy theater-ing. The contestants look universally fucked, and I would bet everything I own that Steve the newspaper editor from Fort Wayne has never gone out for the role of Rum Tum Tugger. Rum Tum Tugger is a piece of shit anyway.

Alex reads the clue: it's about a play that opened for the final time on Broadway in 1915 at the Booth Theatre.

Bruce's eyebrows crowd together as though they are teaming up to deliberate the answer, and the aura of the television makes his face look dark, handsome, and slightly purple, like an old-timey cameo portrait. He guesses *My Fair Lady*, having exhausted the other two options in his repertoire, *Show Boat* and *The Crucible*. It's a real Hail Mary, but all I've got is *Cats*. The answer is something we've never heard of. Nobody else has ever heard of it either.

Sheri has been calling Bruce obsessively. She phones several times a day, seemingly undeterred by his refusal to answer. He hates talking on the phone. And the only thing he hates more than that is getting involved in other people's business. His introversion is buying me a little time, but it won't last long.

"'The Theater!'" Bruce says, smiling at the absurdity of it all, his dimples sinking deep into the softness of his cheeks.

He stands up from the couch, grabs my plate from the coffee table, and takes it with him to the kitchen. He shakes our forks half-heartedly under the faucet and shoves them in the dishwasher. He looks fondly at me, and I take a mental picture because this may be the last time.

I head upstairs. I'm still awake when he settles in beside me. I sit up and we're both leaning against our solid wood headboard that, along with the wooden frame, has supported our marital bed for the past twenty-three years.

"Bruce," I begin, "I know I said Sheri was a little crazy, and I know she's texted and called and everything. She thinks Rob and I are having an affair. That's why she's bothering you. I'm so sorry."

"Oh, so she is a little crazy." His eyebrows lift and wiggle in amusement. "I can just keep ignoring her. I don't really see why that's a problem or how it impacts me."

"It only impacts you . . ." I pause, ". . . if it's true."

He turns, "Is it?"

"Yes, yes, it is. I'm so sorry. I'm so sorry I've done this to you." I stop talking. The room is very silent; it's as if someone has taken his breath away.

"How long?" he asks.

"Two years."

The figure is astonishing to say out loud. The quietness resumes.

I wait for him to yell. But Bruce is not a yeller. I wait for him to get out of bed and storm out of the room. Bruce does not do drama. I wait for him to ask me for a divorce. I wait for all the things I think will happen next but don't.

"Wow. I didn't see that coming," he says.

"Do you want to talk about it?" I ask.

"Not now, no, I don't," he says, and he rolls over on his side, his back to me.

"Are you sure?" I mutter.

Silence.

I can't tell if he's sleeping or fuming or mentally counting dead vice presidents backwards, a trick he does when he wants to bring on sleep.

The moonlight falling over his body looks milky and bluish, like light from a neon sign, and I'm struck by how many times I've seen this exact same thing. His body turned on its side, hinged in several places, clinging to something invisible, something I want more than anything to be me.

He'll be up and gone tomorrow morning before I even stir.

• • •

It's January 22, and the Tahoe pulls up along the front of the house, not to the side like it normally does. Sergeant North, the new head of my detail, is driving. Rob has taken some vacation time. I'm hoping he'll use the week to convince his wife to resume their moderately satisfying routine of dinner club and churchgoing and not go public about the affair. I'm not optimistic.

I need to see Rich, my COO. He's been the backbone of my administration, and I rely on his judgment and advice. The first thing I do when I get to work is pop my head into his office.

"I need to see you before you do anything else this morning. We need to talk."

Rich is cool, calm, and unflappable, even though he's probably on his third cup of coffee. He's likely been here for over an hour, going through emails, making sure the city is on track, making his hard job look easy, and attending to the minutiae and details of running our complex organization.

"Sure," he says and comes around from his standing desk into the center of his office. "Do you want to talk in my office or yours?"

"Here's fine," I say. I pull his office door shut behind me. Closed-door meetings between the two of us are rare. I'm sure the rest of the staff will take notice.

"I think you should sit down for this one," I say, but he declines. Rich is a pacer, not a sitter. He takes long strides back and forth in front of his desk while I take a seat instead, immobilized by the shame, the mess of it all.

I shift and clear my throat, "It's true. I have been having an affair with Rob. Sheri knows and I've told Bruce. It's about to come out. I don't think it's going to stay a secret. We need to put together a strategy and figure out if there's a way to manage all of this."

Rich keeps pacing. This isn't a total surprise to him.

Just last week, after I had finished speaking at the Martin Luther King Jr. Day program at the old Woolworth's building downtown, part of the backdrop of the famous Nashville civil rights sit-ins, Rob had told me he was going to quit, take early retirement, and try to fix things with Sheri. Not a bad plan, but one that would raise eyebrows. We went to Rich and told him Sheri was crazy and making everything up. He knew better than to ask what was true and what wasn't. He suggested Rob take more vacation time.

I wait for Rich to stop moving. I wait for shock and disappointment to stop him, but there is none. Of course I'm a liar. I'm in politics. I'm no different than anyone else who is.

He takes a sip of his coffee and shakes his head a little. "Okay. This is happening. You need to tell Sean immediately."

I nod and open the door. My team collectively smiles up at me. They're happy I'm here. They trust me. They know me. At least, they think they do.

Hostages

I worried it would come to this.

I grew up in a perpetual state of terror that I was a cheater just like my dad. I was always on guard, damn sure to keep that wolf away from my door, catching myself in minor flirtations and then using any leftover contrition from Catholic school to my advantage. I was sure that inside of me lay a secret hereditary ability to betray the people I loved while simultaneously skipping through the world unburdened, guiltless, and free. The appearance of freedom and the experience of freedom are two different things, though. I have never been less free.

My dad had rules about cheating; there was an order, a civility, to it. He shared them with me when I was twenty-two, one drunken night in Breckenridge after a day of skiing. I had watched him cheat on my mom. For a long time, I was perplexed. He was charming. People liked him. Even my mom, knowing everything, had stayed married to him for two decades.

"There are rules, Megan," he slurred. "Rules you should have learned from me a long time ago."

"Like what?" I asked with a laugh.

"Rule Eight. Anytime you throw a party, make sure you have 'fun ice,' you know, the kind you buy from an ice machine—clear, small cubes. I find the drinks always taste better."

I had no idea what this had to do with infidelity, and I was doubtful that the right ice cubes would help attract prospective sexual partners.

"Rule Ten. A good margarita always has a cheap beer in it."

Again, nonsensical. I let him rattle off a few more, half listening.

"Rule Fifteen. Never, ever cheat with someone who doesn't have as much to lose as you do.

"Rule Twenty-Five. Are you listening? If more than one person knows a secret, it won't stay a secret very long. And Rule Twenty-Six— it takes two people to have an affair, so based on Rule Twenty-Five, you're already screwed."

Maybe he already saw the cheater in me. Maybe he already knew that one day I would need these rules. It's also possible he just wanted to regale me and my friends with his life wisdom. Just a few years removed from community theater, he is forever a performer. I remember rattling off his rules back to him one by one, loudly, for all to hear, and then throwing my head back and laughing. For once, he wasn't laughing. I wish I'd paid more attention to Rules Fifteen and Twenty-Five.

• • •

"Bruce is on the phone," Katy says. "Apparently, media trucks are driving by your house. No one has come to the door yet, but he thinks it's just a matter of time. It's a good thing we left."

Katy is a good friend. She's graciously allowed us to use her dining room as mission control while mine is under siege by NewsChannel 5.

When a politician experiences any kind of public humbling, a media shitstorm is to be expected. We're preparing—preparing for a few days of unflattering, many-pored, cross-eyed, viral photographs; preparing for a few speculative articles and salacious headlines in clownish 400-point Helvetica; preparing to be a meme or a third-tier joke on *SNL*. Right now, Sean is preparing me.

"Let's go over the questions Phil's likely to ask," says Sean, emerging from Katy's kitchen and peering momentarily out the window to make sure nobody has found us out.

I've brought in the Machine, from Chicago, where politics is always a dirty business. This is the water they swim in. They show up brazen, unfrazzled, ready to handle messaging, control the narrative, get in and get out.

In a few hours, I have a sit-down with a local reporter, Phil Williams. After Rob's admission to Sheri, there's no point in denying things, so we're trying to stay ahead of them. Phil is getting the exclusive, mostly because he's the one who has been badgering us for public records related to my travel and to my text messages. He gets the scoop, finders keepers. Also, I tend to think he's a decent man. He went on a casual fishing expedition and came home, surprised as all hell, with eight hundred pounds of tuna. I'm sure there's a part of him dreading this as much as I am.

"Just say the affair started after Max died and everyone will forgive you," someone says.

My head is buried in my hands, so I don't see who makes the suggestion, and I'm not sure it matters. The voices and bits of advice are a constant roar in my ears. I haven't been sleeping, and I currently have the intellectual capacity and reflexes of one of my Donald Pliner booties. Just yesterday, Patrick had looked down at my footwear and pointed out I had on a black bootie on my left foot and a blue one on my right. That's exactly how I feel.

The Machine are seated around Katy's dining room table, which is large and as heavily lacquered as they are. They like the Max angle and they're waiting for my response.

"I can't say that," I tell them. "It's not true. I know it may sound ridiculous at this point, but I'm not a liar. I can't say something that isn't true."

I watch their lips momentarily flatten into pink lines of contempt. I'm making their job difficult. The truth will be a real obstacle here.

The group goes back to whispering among themselves. If I won't lie, they'll need to figure out which parts of the real story are the best. We can say I'm grieving—that's true. We can say my marriage has been in trouble for a while—also true. But the reality is that I was lonely, bored, and angry. I had been silently screaming, and finally, the person next to me in the car said, "Hey, I hear you." I let my guard down. It turns out the wolf was inside me all along. The real danger was letting her out.

"Phil is going to ask you if you're still seeing Rob and you need to be honest." Sean's voice drops. "You aren't, are you?"

The muscles in my neck begin to stiffen and I'm itchy, everywhere. I can't tell Sean the truth. I have tried so hard not to involve anyone else in my deception, and yet, here we are. Yes, I'm still seeing Rob. I might love Rob. At the very least, I'm addicted to Rob. Rob is my safe place. Rob's entire life has been blown up, just like mine, and we need each other right now.

As my pause evolves into a certifiable silence, Sean's eyes beg me for an answer—not just any answer, but the right one.

"No," I reply, looking him straight in the eye. "We're not seeing each other."

Now, I am a liar.

Sean is relieved. He believes me. His face softens, as though he's been pinky promised that the seven-foot-tall Mickey Mouse he embraced outside Space Mountain was the real Mickey and not some guy named Trevor who works the fry station at Five Guys on weekends and plays in a ska band.

"I figured," he says. He grins, a glimmer of faith in me returning to his (bloodshot) eyes.

An hour passes in which nearly everybody close to me advises gently against this sit-down. The Machine ask me flat out not to do it. Katy says she can sneak me out the back door. Bruce calls to reiterate the fact that he would not like to be any part of this groveling. And there will be groveling. The entire strategy is groveling.

There's a knock at the door. NewsChannel 5 is here.

"Be *deeply* ashamed, *very* sorry," someone says, "and also, sad. *Very* sad." I head to the bathroom for a makeup touch-up. I see "Weary Willie" when I look in the bathroom mirror, but with waterproof mascara and a better reason to frown.

Phil Williams and the NewsChannel 5 Investigates team filter into Katy's foyer, and she offers them coffee and baked goods. She's being hospitable not because she wants to be but because she's Southern. Underneath her red hair and stylish attire, she is a fiery ball of rage. I'm glad to be here and not at home. I'm happy that she has agreed to host my descent into infamy, which, as everyone knows, takes a true friend.

The voices beyond the bathroom door are friendly and familiar, which leads me to believe that the NewsChannel 5 Investigates team is the same as the regular NewsChannel 5 team and possibly half of the Code Red Weather team too.

I take one last look. I've gone light on the foundation, blush, and everything else. No eyelashes will be curled today. The look is remorseful and haggard. Rest assured, I'm nailing it. Katy knocks and looks at me.

"You look ready." She smiles grimly. "Good luck!"

Notice how she doesn't say I look great.

* * *

Phil and I sit facing each other in stern armchairs with floral brocade bolted down so tightly I wonder if it's tried to escape before. A director fiddles with Katy's curtains and adjusts some of the books on her side table. The whole thing is meant to look informal and comfortable. It didn't register at the time when we planned this interview that Katy's house is cozy but dark. She decorates in the classic English style that women our age love.

Phil clears his throat and wiggles the arms of his suit jacket, catching my eye for just a moment, a moment in which it's abundantly clear that neither of us expected to be here. He has accepted my team's terms for the interview, which were not hard terms to accept. Nothing is off the table. He can ask anything he wants to. He can go for broke. Even he seems unsure as to whether or not that's a good idea.

A young woman adds a final layer of powder to his (already very powdery) nose. The lights come on and are adjusted one way and then tilted the other. Microphones are checked, brought closer, pulled back. We start rolling. I talk first, which, in the interest of controlling the narrative, seems wise.

"I'm a public person, but there are things in my private life I want to talk about today," I begin.

My tone is serious, too serious, and not helped by the fact that my throat is dry and I have to keep swallowing to avoid the feeling that I'm choking. Phil Williams says nothing after this, so I keep going.

"I had an affair. And the affair was between two consenting, middle-aged adults."

I feel myself biting my lip and sweating. Though the Machine forbade neither of those things, I'm sure they're watching the monitors and wishing that they had.

Phil Williams freezes. He says nothing, watching the ship sink herself. My mind is blank. I'm talking about God's forgiveness and

Nashville's forgiveness and how *very* sorry and *deeply* embarrassed I am. I can't stop.

Finally, Phil pipes up to ask how long the relationship went on. I tell him. He asks why I didn't remove Rob from my detail. I tell him that, yes, I should have. He asks fair questions and the whole thing starts to take the shape of the conversation between a repentant teenager and her loving father, which isn't the worst thing it could be. He asks about MeToo, which I explain, and I'm sure will continue to explain, is about hundreds of years of subjugation of women in the workplace. Then, he asks if we used taxpayer dollars to conduct the affair. No, we didn't. Of course we fucking didn't.

Phil would probably win an Emmy if Rob was a publicly funded concubine, but that's not what was going on. They have access to the records. They can see for themselves. Rob didn't bill for more hours than he worked. At least not that I know of, but it's not like I was helping him fill out his timesheet in the postcoital glow. I have never even seen a timesheet. The reason Rob worked a lot is that I worked a lot and that, unlike the Karls and the Bills that came before me, while I was busy working, I was also busy having a vagina. There were more threats against me. There were more vulnerabilities. There were people grabbing me on the street. The police oversaw my security assignments. I needed more protection than the men before me from the men around me.

Phil is leaning hard on his notes, listing the cities Rob and I traveled to together, asserting that some taxpayers are going to feel as though they funded our relationship. I can hear Katy's clock ticking and tocking. Everything in my brain is screaming, *THIS INTERVIEW IS OVER.*

"This is a bad day," I tell him. "I'm going to have a lot more bad days coming up. But I've already had my worst day and I know the difference between a mistake and tragedy. And this is a mistake."

He has just one more question. It's about Bruce and me, which Bruce would hate. Phil Williams has the gall to remind me that I don't have to answer it, that the relationship between me and my husband is between me and my husband. I wish he'd tell that to the other NewsChannel 5 truck currently parked outside my house.

All I say is that I'm lucky to have Bruce's support. It's the one statement I make that I'm not sure is true.

We wrap. I hug Phil Williams, which I'm sure is quite literally the Machine's worst nightmare, along with the fact that I used the word *affair*. Still, not bad for my warm-up.

Now it's time for the full-frontal assault.

"I think it's best if you just walk out and read a statement, not take any questions, and call it a day," says Sean, sitting next to me in the back of the Tahoe. Ten minutes after the NewsChannel 5 truck left, we had started off to the courthouse, where the conference room has been turned into a pressroom so that everyone else can have a piece of me and the story.

"And what about Bruce? Are we picking him up on the way? He's going to stand next to you, right? It'll make a good visual and a strong statement that you have his support," Sean reminds me. I'm sure Sean is feeling sick at this point. He loves Bruce. Bruce and I have hung out with Sean and Whitney, his wife, many times. We got shit-faced and sang karaoke. We were friends.

"Bruce isn't coming," I tell him.

Earlier, when I had told Bruce about the various interviews and mea culpas I was going to have to roll out, he had made one request.

"Please don't ask me to appear with you in any hostage videos. I just don't think I can do it," he had said.

"Hostage video" has always been our shorthand for when a public official acts badly and the aggrieved wife (it is usually the wife) has to stand by her man at the press conference, and look on stoically, while he apologizes profusely to her, his family, and his constituents. We'd always thought of these as particularly pitiful scenes—predictable, smarmy, and disingenuous.

He had looked relieved when I had said I wouldn't make him be a hostage.

I don't want him next to me. Whatever I have to do, I will do alone. I've been on my own since Max died. I will stand before any cameras by myself and confess. No one else needs to stand with me.

We arrive at the courthouse, which is a blinding scene full of over-caffeinated, stressed-out journalists and camera operators who look like they just want to go home. I walk into the "pressroom." Sergeant North stands to my left offstage, the way Rob used to. I refuse a podium. I refuse a canned statement. Instead, I stand before the press to tell them what's happening. I answer all their questions, and then it's over.

I go to bed that night feeling tired but almost peaceful. I did the right thing. There are no more secrets. I admitted to the affair, pledged transparency, and asked for forgiveness. It could be worse. Rob could've been a bank robber or a heroin addict, but he was just lonely. We both were. We were lonely and we cheated. I finally let myself succumb to it, having fought it off for twenty-three years of marriage. I made a mistake. I owned up.

But the problem with having one secret is that people always think you have more.

· · ·

The next morning, just after Sergeant North and I have arrived at the office, my cell phone rings. It's the district attorney. He doesn't like me and, truthfully, I've always thought he was a bit of a putz.

"Mayor, I want to do you a solid," he says brightly, with an audible shit-eating grin on his face I can feel through the phone. "I'm gonna ask the Tennessee Bureau of Investigation to look into things. I want you to have a clean bill of health."

Fuck.

I'm confident that there is nothing the DA would love more than for me to *not* have a clean bill of health. I thank him for letting me know and hang up the phone.

The DA doing me a "solid" is the last thing I need.

A State of Undress

"The chief of police called this morning and needs to see you right away."

It's February 20, and Patrick is standing in my doorway, gaunt, with dark circles under his eyes.

"I'm going to make time on your calendar. I can push a few things. He's on his way over now," he says.

We both know it's not good. Patrick waits patiently for me to react, but I don't. I just shrug my shoulders and roll back and forth in my chair. Secret's out. I confessed already. Everywhere from Smithville, Tennessee, to Singapore, people know I was screwing my security guard. We're cooperating with open records requests and with the DA. We're doing everything we're supposed to do. We ran on transparency, and my promise to the staff has been that that's how we'll keep governing.

The office bustles, but gone is the laughter and joy. We move quickly and precisely, stepping softly around each other at the copier and the coffeepot. The margarita machine, a gift from a constituent, sits gathering dust in the kitchen, a sad reminder of when staff would take it home on a weekend to bust out a little from the workweek. When I was elected as the first female mayor of Nashville, people sent gifts, celebrities visited, and CNN wanted my take on what was happening in Washington, Delhi, and Dubai. *Elle* magazine decided I was a feminine icon and wanted to do a profile. These were the spoils of victory. We'll never say it out loud, but the victory feels like it's slipping away. My second term, which was a no-brainer last month, is a long shot today. All of it is taking a toll.

Poor, loyal, dedicated Sean ages five years for every eight-hour workday, and Patrick is looking too skinny in his skinny pants (which he probably loves). We thought it would be best to manage the crisis internally and project "What crisis?" externally, but shifting from total chaos to Zen Buddhism every time the phone rings is wearing us all out. I've kept making appearances and signing executive orders about trees and sidewalks. I know how to govern. It's the only thing I know how to do right now. I'm not even annoyed when my old friend Opponent A requests my presence at an upcoming ribbon cutting for one of his properties. He has yet to forgive me for winning the election, but in these troubled times, even his lived-in surliness is almost a comfort. Rob has retired. We both decided it would be best if he left before I went on television and publicly humiliated myself. That way, he wouldn't get fired and lose his pension. After being gaslit for over twenty years, the very least Sheri deserves is alimony.

Elease pops her head into my office. Poor Elease. Poor, ever-trusting Elease. This is about killing her. Her face is an awful mix of love and disappointment. She's believed in me, in *us*, since day one. She believes less now. I can see it.

"Do you want me to fix you a coffee while you wait for the chief?" she offers.

I say, "Thank you, Elease," but what I really want to say is:

I'm so, so sorry, Elease.

Please don't lose faith in me, Elease.

I really fucked up, Elease.

I take off my shoes and place my feet on the cool of the concrete, breathing deeply, trying to absorb as much of the bright, beautiful office as I can. I'm not going anywhere, but a part of me wants to hold it all closer—the furniture; the photography; the Crosley record player from Dierks Bentley; the stack of vinyl we liked to play in the mornings, when the mornings felt a little less like funerals; the "We Make Nashville" banners in the common area.

Elease brings the coffee and smiles for just a second, before remembering that I've broken her heart.

The chief shows up in my office ten minutes later. He looks like he might throw up on himself. His face is ashen and covered in a sheen of nervous sweat. He won't stop shifting; he keeps putting his hands on his hips in kind of a carefree way, then dropping them. The chief is not carefree. I'm worried. He glances at a picture of Lady Gaga on my wall like he doesn't quite trust her, and I try to remember if I've ever seen him out of uniform in the two and half years we've worked together.

I offer him a chair in my "collaboration zone," but he'd rather stand. Whatever he's here to tell me, he wants to do it quickly and leave. He looks side to side like we're being tailed, reaches into his pocket, and pulls out a small thumb drive. My stomach sinks. I have no idea what could be on it, but when a police officer hands you a thumb drive, you can assume it's got something fairly incriminating on it.

"Ma'am," he says, clearing his throat, "when Rob retired, we took possession of his work computer. My tech guys tell me there's something he saved that you need to know about."

He looks down and starts shifting again.

"I haven't seen it—I want you to know that—but I do think you need to call your lawyer. We got a subpoena request from the DA this morning and we're going to honor it."

A long, labored exhale I can feel ten feet away escapes from his nose as he readies himself for the hard part.

"The tech guys tell me that there are two pictures of a woman . . . in a state of undress. Like I said, I haven't seen them, but . . ."

He doesn't have to finish. He is clearly mortified that he even has to deliver this news, let alone imagine that his boss may or may not have removed her clothes to pose for naked pictures.

Rob, you son of a bitch.

I smile politely. "Thank you, Chief."

I fan my fingers toward the door like a QVC hostess and he shuffles out of the office.

As soon as I see him on the sidewalk out the window, I start yelling.

"Elease! Get Jerry Martin on the phone, *please*. Tell him I need to see him as soon as possible."

She pops her head up from her desk, nods, and goes to work.

• • •

Jerry's office is just down the street from the courthouse, so it doesn't take him long to arrive. He's a former US attorney, and I trust him. He's a great lawyer and a good man, the kind you'd have save your floundering political career and then have over for beers later.

"The police chief just came to see me and handed me this." I take the thumb drive out of my pocket and hand it to him. I'm shaking.

"He says there are naked pictures on it. I need you to take the drive some place safe and see what we're dealing with. I can't believe I have to ask you to do this. I'm so embarrassed and I can't fucking believe it. Goddamn Rob."

Jerry doesn't react with the shock and awe I expect. Maybe it's because he's worked in politics long enough that he already has a dedicated space in his office for thumb drives like this one. I might be a woman, but as far as political leaders go, I haven't chosen a unique path to implosion. A few days ago, Trump's attorney Michael Cohen admitted to paying hush money to cover up the president's alleged affair, which he heatedly denies. Deny, deny, deny.

"Let me take this to my office," he says. "I'll come back after I'm done. Don't worry, Mayor, it's going to be okay."

I walk him out into the waiting area, where he gives me a too-bright smile and heads out the door.

Patrick meets me when I'm halfway back to my office; he's flipping through the white pages of my schedule, knowing that we'll have to clear my afternoon.

"It looks like you've got a couple of meetings I can push, or I can ask someone on staff to take some for you. I'll handle it. Don't worry," he says and gives me the same too-bright smile Jerry just did.

It's the second time in less than five minutes I've been told not to worry. So of course, that's exactly what I begin to do.

* * *

Jerry comes back in less than an hour, and this time he brings a second attorney with him, Dave Garrison. They're law partners and have been doing this for a long time. Elease seats them in my office. We shut the door. I don't invite any additional staff to join us, something that in two and half years I've rarely ever done.

"How bad is it?" I ask, pacing, biting the inside of my lips. I'm a pacer now too.

"I think we can manage this. It's two pictures of a woman in a state of undress," Jerry says. He uses five words to avoid saying "naked."

"*But*," he says, thrusting a finger into the air to prepare for the grand unveiling of the bright side, "you can't see a face. There's no way to tell who's in the picture, and it *is* clear that whoever is being photographed is not aware of the camera."

I'm livid. Rob and I had always agreed: no pictures, no evidence, no trail to follow. My breathing shallows and my face gets hot. Jerry keeps talking, but I hardly notice.

When had he taken the pictures?

In Washington when I was changing between meetings?

In San Francisco when I was nauseous and needed to lie down?

I sure as fuck didn't give him permission.

Dave, I'm guessing the more techie one, chimes in to explain that the photos were recovered from Rob's computer, not his phone. He'd taken the pictures with his phone, and if he had just left them there, they would have disappeared when he wiped it. But because God put more energy into Rob's cheekbones than his frontal lobe, he emailed them to himself. He emailed them to a *secure police server, where things never get erased.* The pictures will live on longer than I will. Sure, it'll be illegal to publish them outright, but they'll be fair game for public records requests by the media and for anything the DA decides to do.

For a few more minutes, the men try to reassure me, all without saying the word *naked*. I tell them I don't want to see the pictures. I don't want to know if it's me. In perfect unison, they say "Don't worry" one more time and leave. I rub my temples and get ready to tell Sean. I reason with myself. It's just blurry pictures. People already know Rob and I were together. It doesn't matter.

But the pictures do matter. A naked woman always matters.

● ● ●

The media is a collection of mostly good people, people with families and rescue dogs, people who recycle their glass bottles and wave hello to their neighbors. Together, though, chasing leads, competing, trying to get a scoop, these good people become a very bad thing. News gets out about the photos the next day, and the press rejoices. Whether or not they can circulate the photos is unimportant—the fact that they exist is enough to turn me from an adulterer into a whore. I'm on the front page of the paper, the editor having decided to use the most unflattering photo they have of me. I look like I am jaundiced and have seven chins. This is my fall from grace, live on the scene.

Phil Williams, accidental redeemer of justice and truth, dissects the contents of the photos pixel by pixel on the evening news, hoping, praying, begging for the "woman in a state of undress" to be me. Analysts try to decide if the purse in the lewd photographs (Gadzooks! A clue!) is a purse I've been photographed with before. It goes on all week. CNN picks up the scent, and then, the tabloids overseas. The throngs of people at the grocery store who used to cheer for me as I bought arugula and ask for my autograph at checkout won't even meet my eye. Online, my supporters go dark, not even bothering to respond to their out-of-town relatives who boast that they knew "right from the beginning" that I was the wrong choice. The very reason I think my people will stick by me is the same reason they don't. They're human. I'm human, I made a terrible mistake, I owned up. As the #MeToo movement rockets along, nobody cares that the pictures in question were taken without consent. Nobody cares that the relationship was between two consenting, age-appropriate adults with no interns in sight. Nobody cares what's true and what's not. Especially not the DA.

The pictures don't make my mistake into a tragedy—they make it into a scandal. News trucks camp outside our house and the courthouse.

They follow Bruce to work, lurking menacingly behind his bicycle. The dogs give them hell the way I wish I could.

On February 22, NewsChannel 5 airs security footage of the Tahoe driving through the cemetery off Fourth Avenue, the place I would go in the mornings to drink my coffee and be with my thoughts. The place Bruce and I plan to have Max interred. The days of "controlling the narrative" are over. Suddenly, *Inside Edition* is running a story that Rob and I were having sex there. Is she an adulterer *and* a necrophiliac?

We go from one step ahead of the press to five steps behind them. But it's no longer about me. It's about clickbait and network ratings, adrenaline and dopamine. One headline says I'm blowing the fire department. Another alleges that since I've been sleeping with a cop, I must be working with the cops too. Phil Williams, bless his heart, gets a lead that my son's ashes have already been scattered in Colorado. If all of Max is in Colorado, then the cemetery rumors must be true! He finds travel records, contacts my friends, and dives deep, deep, deep into footage of the Tahoe driving in and driving out. I hate seeing him like that, but I know how easy it is to go from decent to totally shameless under the right conditions. Finally, against the advice of the Machine, I put Phil out of his misery, emailing to let him know some of Max is in Colorado and the rest is in Nashville, waiting to be interred at the cemetery. I also let him know that he's an asshole.

● ● ●

Bruce doesn't know if he wants to be my husband, so he becomes my strategist instead. He's coolheaded and removed. As a PR guru draws a series of concentric circles filled with "next steps" and "what ifs" and scenarios A through G on our whiteboard, Bruce listens intently and offers feedback, talking about the affair like it's the collapse of a stranger's career, not our marriage. He asks me what I think, willing to consult but not converse with me. He caps and uncaps his Expo markers. He makes another pot of coffee. If he's heartbroken, or hurt in any way, he doesn't let it show. There is no discussion about me moving from the bed to the couch, no feeling that he's lawyered up. Really, there's no feeling at all. I'm not sure I have any right to be hurt by it, but I am.

"Do you want to talk about it?" I ask him, meekly, in our few moments of quiet.

Invariably, it's a no.

He'll fight for the administration. But I'm not so sure he's up to fight for us. I'm not sure I'll fight for either.

The TBI has been digging around and they've already subpoenaed my phone. They're a little late to the party as I've already received a letter from Sheri's lawyers warning me not to delete anything that might be material for her to use in a divorce.

The DA is sure that he has something he can charge me with, though none of us have any idea what it could be. Rob and I agree to keep a distance, continuing to talk infrequently on burner phones. He feels shitty about the pictures (I just compartmentalize, choosing to believe that they aren't me). Neither of us saw it going this way. Both of us are sorry. Of course, it's too late to fix it.

• • •

"I think we should fight this," I say.

Jerry and Dave don't look up. It's the first Sunday in March and we've ordered Greek food for a late dinner. We've been trying to put out fires for weeks. We're failing. I've always been good at rallying support, keeping hope alive, energizing the people.

I don't think I have people anymore.

Team Megan Barry is huddled around the dining room table poking at Styrofoam containers full of gyros and moussaka. Everybody is sullen and gray-faced. Nobody is sleeping. I can see them giving up as they dunk their triangular hunks of pita into the hummus. It's over.

"Why is he doing this to me?" I mutter to nobody in particular.

I don't even know who *he* is anymore. *He's* the DA and Rob and Phil Williams and the other Phil Williamses of the world and even Bruce, who still won't talk to me.

Jerry and Dave have been trying to negotiate with the DA and have just come back from another stalemate. We're on round three of trying to work out a deal, but the DA has broken promise after promise. I am reminded that he is capricious and vindictive and untrustworthy, that this could take time, and that for him, this all seems to be personal.

At one point, the DA wanted funding I didn't give him, and apparently, he was the victim of a thousand other slights I never knew about. Maybe he's still hanging onto a grudge? Either way, it's clear that I'm big game now.

The DA thinks he's got enough evidence to prove the affair involved a misuse of public funds. Maybe it did, but I sure as hell didn't know about it. I never saw a timesheet. I've never had anything to do with billing. I assume Rob's timecards reflect that truth, that we worked all the time.

"What did he say? What does he want me to do?"

Jerry moves across the table to sit next to me and begins, "Before we tell you your options, there's something else you need to know. Rob was in over the weekend. He gave a federal proffer. Do you know what that is?"

I don't even know where "in" is.

"I have no idea. What the fuck is a federal proffer?" I ask, stabbing at my salad, not believing that there could be yet another element of this investigation I don't understand.

Jerry leans in. "It's kind of like being queen for a day. You can put all of your illegal activity on the record, and depending on the kind of deal you've struck, you won't be charged with anything."

Fucking Rob. We had a deal. I will take the heat. I will be the bad guy. I was the one in power, and I crossed the line. He can just walk away, move to Florida, buy a goddamned Jet Ski, play some golf. But he doesn't trust me anymore. Our contact has been limited. There are a dozen hungry reporters parked outside my house *and* his now. It's not like we can have a porch sit and work all of this out together.

"What does that have to do with the investigation?" I needle them. "I didn't do anything illegal. I was immoral, sure, but last I checked, committing adultery isn't a crime in Tennessee. I confessed, for God's sake. I'm totally owning this. Fuck!"

I slam my hand on the table. Everyone jumps. Even Bruce looks surprised.

Jerry rifles through words in his head, careful to select the ones that will offer the most amount of clarity with the least amount of pain.

"Mayor, part of Rob's plea includes a multi-page document of every time, date, and place you both ever had any kind of physical contact. And that's not the worst part."

Jesus Christ.

I close my eyes, trying to remember if any of the sex we had was even worth writing about. It was pedestrian, lusty at best, but there are some things my husband doesn't need to know. And then there's Sheri, poor, rightfully pissed-off Sheri. I brace myself against the dining chair for what comes next.

"What's the worst part?" I ask.

"He says you *expected* him to have sex with you," Jerry says matter-of-factly. "He says you made him do it."

I grab for the burner phone, my fingers trembling and covered in green goddess dressing. After weeks of humiliation and slander and lies, I am truly hurt for the first time. Somebody I trusted lied to me. Somebody who said they loved me, abandoned me. I need to talk to him because I need to *scream* at him.

Jerry gently places his hand over mine and uncurls my fingers from the burner phone.

"It's not what you did, it's what you do next that can land you in jail," he says.

Jail?

My hand goes limp, and I give up with the rest of them.

"You can't have any more contact with him. Are we clear? Assume that any conversation he wants to have from now on is being taped. He is not your friend, and he's not going to help you in any way. It's over."

I repeat it to myself. *He is not my friend. He is not my friend. He is not my friend.*

Prison Clothes

Stacy arrives at the house carrying her makeup kit and a hair dryer. It's early, about 6 AM. The street is dark, still, and frigid, protected by a thin membrane of frost.

"How are you?" she asks, brows contracting into two worried zags. She's been my go-to hair and makeup artist for a long time.

"So-so," I shrug. She was probably expecting a statement of "deep outrage," but I'm too tired for that. I never get to be something as neutral as "so-so."

Stacy wants to hug me but doesn't.

"Where should I set up?" she asks. "Do you want me in your bathroom or in the kitchen?"

Bruce is still upstairs. I don't want to impose on him any more than I already have. Jerry and Dave were here until 2 AM and he needs to get some sleep. Also, I don't want him watching as I select the perfect shoes and hairstyle for my undoing. I'm ashamed of what I've done to him, the position I've put us in, not to mention the entire city.

I tell Stacy the lighting is better in the kitchen.

She nods and immediately gets to work, laying out her brushes and gels on the counter and fiddling with the barstool, positioning it so the

171

sun won't shine in my eyes when it rises on what will be a very, very bad day.

The last time we set up in the kitchen like this, Stacy was doing my hair and makeup for the Country Music Association Awards. My sisters were in town. We giggled and drank champagne while she gave us all elegant shadows under our cheekbones and stuck fake eyelashes on our lids. None of those today.

"Big day?" she asks.

I don't know how much to tell her. Once I let the words take form, it'll be real.

"In a few hours, I'm going to appear before a judge, plead to a felony, and resign." I sigh.

There. It's been said. I am resigning. *I am resigning.*

Stacy freezes, reboots, continues.

"Okay," she says, nodding. "Well then, what's the look we're going for?"

"Innocent," I say.

Pushing the stack of bracelets she wears on her right arm up to her elbow, Stacy begins smearing foundation across the bridge of my nose with a small pink sponge.

The light out the window shifts, and my entire field of vision is white heat. I need to squint.

"Look up," Stacy says, "and try not to smudge your shadow if you want this to last all day."

I squint anyway. A news van parks outside, waiting to see what today will bring. The camera guy hops out for a cigarette, leaning on the bumper and blowing idiotic smoke rings into the abyss.

"They're here early," Bruce remarks on his way down the stairs.

He walks into the kitchen and nods at Stacy, barely glancing my way, picking up the choreography of "normal morning" easily. He pours a cup of black coffee and lets the dogs out. He evaluates the front page of the paper and charges his phone. We still haven't talked about the affair.

The pups linger by the fence, wagging their tails, hoping someone from CNN has a rawhide chew. They've become accustomed to the news crews—the camera people and boom operators milling around outside the boundary of our fence, chatting, drinking their Starbucks, and leaving the empties for us to pick up each night. The dogs don't even bark anymore.

"Do you need me?" Bruce asks before heading back upstairs.

Yes, I need you. I need you to be with me today. I needed you yesterday, three weeks ago, last year. I have needed you for an unimaginable, incommunicable length of time.

"Nah." I smile at him. "I'm okay."

Stacy and I decide on pink lipstick, a shade most often spotted on grandmothers and virgins. She removes the lid from the lipstick with a satisfying pop and vets it one more time, confirming that pink can work nicely for an adulterous felon's skin tone too.

I tilt my chin to her and part my mouth, feeling young and suddenly timid. Slowly, she draws the waxy stain across my lips and holds up a pristine, perfectly circular mirror so I can see whether I look beautiful, powerful, or scared. I look all three. My mouth is the color of the cherry blossom trees that ring the Nashville Metro Courthouse. I pause and rub my lips together. The color is familiar. I remember Rob frantically blotting it off the lapel of his suit so his wife wouldn't notice later. I remember not really giving a shit, thinking it was his problem.

It's my problem now.

I look over at the clock on the oven. 7:04 AM. Time to get dressed.

My closet is dark and filled with the freshness of dryer sheets. I turn on the light and shuffle through the simple sheaths and skirts.

They are almost all the same, but today I'm overwhelmed by blue versus black, pants versus skirt, stockings or no stockings.

I want to ask Bruce what he thinks, but he's never cared what I put on my body. Unless I can convince him that Calvin Klein was a spy for Brezhnev, he never will. But I've never told him that I needed him to care, that I've never stopped trying to impress him. It's felt too personal to say out loud.

I pull a black shift dress from the deck but decide my navy skirt suit is somber enough but less stricken with grief. I wore it for my first State of Metro address. Peter Frampton opened for me, crooning, "Baby, I love your way," and melting my inner teenager as we shared the same stage.

Max's old baseball glove is wedged into one of my open shelves, nestled in with my old bras. It's one of the first things I see when I'm getting dressed in the morning. I smile at it like he's cradled somewhere in the folds of the leather, miniature and resting.

Max.

I've resisted the temptation to wonder what he would think about all of this, but I know. He would hate it. He'd tell me I was a jerk for cheating on Bruce, but then he would tell me he was sorry about all of it. And he would be sorry. He would tell me to blow off the whole court thing. He'd gently scold the reporters for aggravating the dogs and tell them to leave. And because Max was Max, the reporters might actually listen. For a moment, I imagine him out there talking to them in his signature Nike shorts, his warm body steaming in the early-morning chill; they chat and smile, and the press admits to being "uncool." They drive off without leaving a single Starbucks cup behind.

Max would make them want to be better. He made me want to be better. He'd be mad, but he'd forgive me. We were all so good at forgiving each other once.

"Megan, your ride's here!" Bruce calls from the hallway. Sergeant North is outside, waiting.

I zip up my blue suede booties, straighten my skirt, and check myself in the bathroom mirror one last time. The next time I pose for a photo, it will be my mug shot.

Stacy is busy putting away her various paints and potions as I clatter down the stairs and find my way into the kitchen.

She looks up and smiles. "All good? Do you need anything else?"

"Just one last thing. How do I look?"

I have to ask.

"Innocent," she says. Mission accomplished.

* * *

Sergeant North is waiting outside my house in the same white Tahoe that has taken me to and from work for the past two and half years.

I open the car door myself and climb in as several cameras click and questions I pretend not to hear are flung my way. Usually, I'm carrying my purse, a second bag with all my cosmetics, and possibly a third bag filled with things I will not use but always hope to—a hilariously large Nalgene water bottle, workout clothes, a tiny shampoo. Sergeant North notices I'm traveling light, and his eyes linger (but in a decidedly not sexual way).

He hands me the schedule. Our fingers do not touch. The mornings of electricity with Rob are already receding from my memory.

"Busy day," he says brightly. He tries to be bright, always.

"Actually, change of plans." I sigh, looking at the paper, at what life should be. "We aren't doing any of this. We're heading straight into the office. I'll explain while we drive, but first I need to make a call."

I pull out my phone and dial Jerry. We're waiting on the DA to approve our plea so we can get all of this over with. Jerry answers with a flat "hello."

"I'm headed to the office. What's the plan?" I ask. "I need to prep my team. Do we have a plea agreement? We need something in writing from the DA, right?"

Poor Jerry. I have never asked him one question at a time.

"Well, Mayor, you get to choose—you can plead to theft or to official misconduct, but before you decide, let me tell you what each one means."

I stop him. "No need to explain. I'm not pleading guilty to theft. I didn't steal anything. I had an affair, for fuck's sake. I'm guessing that's official misconduct."

Sergeant North bristles. We're not yet close enough that I can casually drop a "for fuck's sake." And we won't be getting close.

"Ma'am," he whispers, "do I need to tell the guys you aren't going to be at the first event today?"

I nod and return to Jerry.

"Look," he reasons, "if you take a plea for official misconduct, the consequences are severe. You'll be a felon for life. There won't be any reprieve, ever. You'll never be able to run for office again, or vote, or, if it matters, own a handgun. You'll have to make sure you're never in the room with another felon or you could go to jail. Think about all of that for a minute."

Confessing publicly and asking for forgiveness five weeks ago seems so quaint now.

"If you go with theft, we can enter into a conditional plea. You can run for office again someday if you want; you maintain your right to vote, and in three years, after you complete your probation, we can have your record expunged. Rob is going to plead guilty to theft. He is going to say he billed for more hours than he worked."

"Great," I scoff.

I can hear the whining in my voice. I hate it. I pull down the passenger-side mirror and dab at the tears welling up in the corners of my eyes, blinking hard. I've got hours to go, and my makeup needs to stay put.

Jerry continues, drawing something up in real time for the DA and reading it off to me. "Are you okay with this language? 'Had this case gone to trial, witnesses are available who would testify that between March 2016 and January 2018, Megan Barry caused over $10,000 but less than $60,000 of metro Nashville city funds to be expended unlawfully to Rob Forrest.'"

Is this how the criminal justice system works? Spitballing on the way to the courthouse? Writing our own plea agreement? Is this normal?

If Rob's prepared to stand up in court and say he billed for more overtime than he really worked, then I guess I'm responsible for those funds being unlawfully expended. I trusted him to bill for the hours he worked, the way I would any employee.

Ah, I had trusted him. The cool "Call me Megan" mayor was so naïve.

I crack a window. It's freezing out, but I don't care.

Something isn't sitting right.

"Jerry, what's with the range for the theft—between $10,000 and $60,000? Have they even completed an audit?" I ask.

He clears his throat. I've noticed he does this before saying something he knows is going to upset me.

"Because for it to be a felony, the amount has to be more than $10,000. The DA is saying you stole $11,000. He wants you to be a felon."

"What a total fucking asswipe," I say.

Sergeant North blushes.

• • •

We pull into the courthouse through the Batcave and immediately press the button to close the garage door. The press has been camped out for days. The last thing we need is somebody sneaking in and making their way up to the office.

I walk up the stairs with Sergeant North three paces behind and peek through the open doors and into the empty offices. The usual hum and bustle of the place is gone. My staff is gathered in the conference room waiting. My office shades are drawn. No sunlight pours through the big glass windows I fell in love with. It feels darker now than when I first arrived.

I join my team in what was the office of the last six mayors: the mayor who was drunk by noon, the mayor who went on *Phil Donahue* and proclaimed his love for his new fiancée while still married to his wife, the other mayors who cheated on their wives, all men. I had believed I was different, so I had chosen a different office.

Sean is standing, shifting his weight back and forth. Claudia is chewing on her lower lip.

"You don't have to resign," she says. "We can weather this. It's all going to be okay. We can get through it."

Her eyes are pleading. I know we can't survive it. She does too. Everyone else looks up at me hopefully.

"Let me tell you how the rest of the morning is going to go," I begin, "and please know, I need y'all to be strong. I've loved serving with you, and at the end of this day, you'll still be here. The work you're doing doesn't go away and neither will you. This city deserves what it's always had from all of you—your willingness to show up and make a difference. I just won't be here to lead you anymore."

Elease looks angry. I've never seen her look angry before. Nobody was expecting this. They thought we would fight it together, that we would win together.

"In about twenty minutes, I'm going across the street to plead guilty. As part of that plea agreement, I'm offering up my resignation. I'll come back over here and do a media avail. I'll read a statement and that'll be it. I'll be gone. I'm going to miss this job and I'm going to miss all of you. I am so, so sorry. Thank you. For everything."

I don't leave time for questions or comments. I leave them to figure out the details of what comes next.

● ● ●

The court is right across the street and driving there is ridiculous, but Sergeant North insists that there is no way we can get there on foot. The press is everywhere. It'll be a free-for-all. Jerry and Paul, another lawyer, scrunch into the back of the Tahoe with me. I sandwich myself in between them so nobody can take pictures. When Rob ordered the car, he had requisitioned additional tint for the windows, making it harder to see in and get photos. Unlike me, it was designed for this.

The judge has cleared his docket and the courtroom in anticipation of my arrival. They're ready for me. We pull into the private parking lot around back, and since I'm not familiar with the inner workings of the courts, my lawyers guide me down the hall to a waiting room. There's an armed, uniformed guy in the room with me. "Not one of ours," Rob would have said. He had taught me how to tell who a Metro Nashville Police officer was and who wasn't. This guy is chatty.

Within ten minutes, I learn he's a court officer, originally from Florida. He's gone through some bad times—cheating and a divorce—and

179

he's had a run-in or two with the law. He's put his life back together. He smiles at me. "You will too. You're too good a person to let this bring you down."

I smile back. I don't feel like a good person. I feel nothing. I haven't felt anything since Max died.

Jerry pops his head into the room a few minutes later. "You're going to stay in here until the case is called. Then, we'll walk in together. The judge will ask you several questions under oath. He's only letting one TV station in the court and only one photographer. Otherwise, the court will be empty."

Thank Christ.

When it's time, the court officer escorts me out.

"Can I give you a hug?" I ask him.

I don't know why I say it. Doing shit like this, getting close, being a human, is how I ended up in this mess.

"Sure," he says, wrapping me up, big, steady, and kind. Not quite Max, but maybe some part of him.

The judge's staff fight back tears as I walk by. It didn't occur to me until now that other people would mourn this loss like I do. I hug all of them too. At this point, what the hell.

Filing into the courtroom, I see the district attorney. He reaches out to either shake my hand or hug me. It's unclear what his lunge signifies, but I turn away. Today, I hate him for many reasons. Of all the injustices in the city, the state, and the world to contend with, he's chosen this. We could have done so much good work together. I look at him and see what I think is shame.

The courtroom smells old and clinical, part hospital, part library. I raise my hand and swear to tell the truth.

"Have you been coerced or blackmailed in any way to take this plea?" says the judge.

I hesitate. I sure feel coerced. If I don't take the plea, the DA is going to read aloud and in detail the specifics of my sex life. My entire team will be deposed. Bruce and I will be broke.

"No, your honor," I say.

I look directly at the DA, angry. He turns away this time. A sole photographer captures this moment and I picture the headlines. "She's not really sorry," they will posit.

My face feels hot and I'm sure it's blotchy. I'm putting all my energy into not crying. The judge is talking, but I don't listen, I don't look, I just wait until it's done. The gavel smacks and an officer leads me to a holding cell. It had never occurred to me that I would have to go to *actual* jail. The sheriff will be very pleased. When I first came into office, he wanted blue police lights added to his car. I informed him that blue lights were reserved for actual law enforcement and pointed out that he just ran a corrections center. I'm now going to have some quality time to reevaluate my position.

• • •

"Please step over here and take off any valuables," the woman at the desk says with a smile. She's young and bubbly—with a spray of freckles, tight cylindrical curls, and Invisalign. She looks like a member of the pep squad, the class president of jail, or something. I'm being processed by Punky Brewster.

"Are you wearing shoes with laces? If not, you can keep 'em on. You can put your rings and earrings in this here bag, and I'll give it all back to you when you're done," she chirps.

"Sure." I slide a silver bracelet off my wrist and remove my wedding ring, twisting it over my knuckle. I'm not sure if or when I'll put it back on.

"There's gonna be some paperwork to sign . . . ," she says and then pauses. "Ma'am, I just can't believe you're standing right here. *Right* in front of me!"

Her colleague chimes in. She's in her early seventies with white, cloud-shaped hair.

"Honey, we all feel so awful about this. Gosh, you're more beautiful in person. The cameras and the TV just don't do you justice. Don't you agree, Sammy?"

Sammy, the bubbly one, nods. "I think what they're doin' to you is a crying shame. If I had my cell phone with me, I'd ask if we could get a selfie. I just can't believe you're here!"

They gush for a handful of seconds and reluctantly hand me off to another officer to complete my processing. She does not gush. She's professional and indifferent, probably not Sammy and Cloud's biggest fan.

"I'm going to take three pictures, one of you facing the camera and then two side photos. I need you to look straight above at that dot," she instructs. "I'll tell you when to turn for the other two."

"Well, I'm hoping we can take a couple and I can choose which one looks best," I say, trying to be funny, likable, electable, sparkly.

There is no humor here.

"Absolutely not, no ma'am. It's one and done, so make it good."

She takes my fingerprints using a reader and enters my name, address, date of birth, height, and weight into the system, typing quickly.

"Okay, it looks like we have all the rest of the information we need. We'll put you in a cell. You aren't allowed to have anything with you during this time besides your paperwork."

I nod, and an officer escorts me into the cellblock.

The jail is exactly like TV jail. Two levels. Commotion. Hollering. Clanking. Several of the other inmates call down to me.

"Hey, MAY-OR! Up here! We was all rootin' for ya. We love you!" a voice says.

I smile and wave. Political reflexes die hard.

"We're not putting you in with the general population," the corrections officer informs me. "You'll have a cell this way."

We walk to a windowless block of cells.

I sit on the edge of a cold bench, and my jailer locks the door. I spend an indeterminate length of time reading the sheet of paper listing my valuables. One side is in English and the other side, Spanish.

A newcomer opens the cell door. "I'm just checking in on you. You okay? Need water, the toilet? It's taking a little longer to process you. It's probably going to be another hour or so."

"No worries. I'm all good. I'm practicing my *español*," I say, glancing at the list of Spanish words on my paper: *un pendiente, un anillo, una billetera.*

I close my eyes and lean back against the cold, dingy tile on the wall, imagining being here for years.

Would time like that make me even more sorry about the pain I caused?

Would I be better?

Do I belong here?

I don't want to think about it. I go back to reading the Spanish words aloud, listening to my voice ricochet off all the hard corners of the space. Occasionally, I stop to stare into the drain in the middle of the concrete floor, there to flush away God knows what.

An hour or so later, the cell door swings open again, and an officer appears.

"We're done. You're free to go. I just need you to sign the release form."

I glance at the sheet, doing a quick scan to make sure the information is correct.

"Wait, my birthday's wrong—you've made me older than I am. And you're kidding—it says I weigh forty more pounds than I actually do! Can you fix that?"

I catch the eye roll.

"It'll take me several hours to reprocess the paperwork if you want it changed. And you'll have to wait back in the holding cell."

"Forget it." I sigh. My public record just got older and fatter. Every woman's nightmare.

• • •

When I walk out into the sunlight, the press is pushing up against the chain-link fence outside the building, hoping, I guess, for several more photos of this day. I wonder what they'll do when this day is over.

Sergeant North and a couple of other cops on my detail hustle me into the car. This time, I sit in the front. Fuck the press. Let them take all the pictures they want.

"Are you guys hungry? I'm starving. And I really want Mexican food. Let's go for lunch. On me," I say.

So we do.

It's relatively jovial and they all get enchiladas. We talk about family and babies and interesting things we've done over the past two and half years. We do not talk about the fact that I was just in the slammer or that I had sex with their boss on multiple, well-documented occasions.

"I'm sorry things ended this way," I tell them, just before the check comes. These guys were good to me. They trusted me and I betrayed them.

Had any of them ever suspected? I wonder.

They were Rob's direct reports, and respecting hierarchy is baked into policing processes and relationships. If they had known, they never would have said anything.

Around 1:45, I settle up. The officers need to get back to the office. I don't need to be anywhere, but I also don't have a car.

"Sergeant North, can you take me home? I think it's still okay. I'm the mayor until 5 PM today and it's only 2 PM. I promise, it's the last thing I need you to do for me."

"Sure, ma'am," he says with a smile.

We ride from East Nashville to the west side, through the still-bad traffic, listening to classic rock on the radio. Bob Seger's "Like a Rock" comes pouring through the speakers. I've got the volume turned way up. I'm singing. At this point, why the hell not?

Sergeant North pulls up alongside the house and looks at me, misty-eyed.

"Ma'am. You are like a rock. This song is about you. You're going to be okay."

I hope that he's right.

I collect my stuff and shut the door to the Tahoe for the last time. There is one lone news crew parked across the street. I walk over and give them all a hug. Then, I go inside the house and wipe the makeup off my face. And it's done.

Hip Waders and Fly Rods

The walk toward Concourse B is not one that I relish. People are staring—the woman at the gate pouring $12 trail mix into the cup of her hand, the man in the gray suit drinking a Michelob Ultra at the airport Tootsies at 9 AM, the girl at Hudson News considering a small bear in a shrunken Music City T-shirt. They are all staring. I catch glimpses of myself too, flashing across random television screens, on a coffee-soaked sheet of newsprint peeking out of the teeming trash can. What a feeling it is to be yesterday's top story and today's old news.

Pale-legged passengers arriving from Houston pour out of the boarding bridge and onto the dizzying geometric expanse of BNA carpet, featuring visually unappealing shades of brown and looking like a drawing Picasso might have made in childhood while fever-stricken and delirious. I didn't think the throng would notice me, but collectively, they do, whispering, gawking, trying not to gawk, which is painfully awkward and much worse. I take in a parade of expressions—shock, pity, sadness, amusement—and pretend to take a call. It was gently suggested to me that the airport with no security a few days after my resignation might be an unwise choice, but I made it anyway. Katy advised that I wear some kind of disguise, but I didn't have the audacity. Or the right wig. I make it to the gate feeling hot in the face and exhausted and nab a seat overlooking the runway. A little girl plays with a stuffed pony while her mother pokes at her iPhone. I smile at her, happy to be anonymous to someone, and then pry open my own off-brand Chex mix. It only cost $8.95.

I'm going to visit my little sister, Heather, in Belgrade, Montana, originally a railroad town named after the capital of Serbia in honor of the original Serbian investors. They still celebrate the high school home-coming with a fall festival and a football game. If there's a place to hide out in the world, it's there. And if someone travels to this part of Montana without hip waders and a fly rod, you can assume they're disappearing.

Heather's family is on spring break. She's a schoolteacher, and her friends are schoolteachers. From what I've discerned, none of them give a shit about the politics of the Mid-South. Her husband, Kurt, man-ages the golf club. He's smart and introverted, usually a man of few words, all of them excessively kind. The offenses I've committed have likely been lumped in with the rest of the local gossip.

"You heard that Randall has a drinking problem?"

"You heard that Marsha's son is moving to the city?"

"You heard Heather's sister down in Nashville had an affair?"

Belgrade is a small, insular planet. My news will be nothing but a quick stop midway through a morning cup of coffee. Thank God for small towns.

Bruce texts:

All checked in?

I text back:

Yep

We've established that we're concerned about each other's general health and well-being, but little beyond that. I don't know if he wants to be married to me. I don't know if I want to be married to him. And I'm still in touch with Rob, which helps no one. Sheri filed for divorce in February, but the announcement hasn't caused me to rush into his arms to live out my pedestrian fantasies of Saturday matinees at AMC, Sunday football, and stuffing jalapeño poppers together. I'm mad at Rob. I don't know if or why he lied to the DA, but I know that I trusted him, and he hurt me. He cost me everything. But I cost him everything too. Our continuing text barrages aren't helping anything. Was it real? Were we real? Neither of us knows.

"Good morning, Delta passengers!" the agent at the desk calls out with too-bright radio DJ enthusiasm. My fellow travelers assemble single file with their boarding passes and carry-ons in hand. The little girl's mother looks up from her phone and a flush hits her cheeks as she recognizes me. She grabs her daughter's hand hurriedly and they head to the gate with the others. I decide I'll wait.

I step into the airplane, immediately submerged in the low-pitch purr of the engine, the closing and opening of overhead bins, the whistle of strange plastic nipples next to the reading light that shoot cool air at your face. The flight is full, warm, and already musty. People shift in their seats and fiddle with the windows, occasionally glancing up to consider the question *Is it really her?*

After checking my boarding pass, the flight attendant throws me a sympathetic glance that says, "Best of luck!" I push my sunglasses up and muster the courage to walk the length of carpeted runway to my seat, which is somewhere near the back of the plane. The good news is that after the *Tennessean*'s coverage and Twitter, these folks can't even begin to compete in the cruelty department.

With breath that's shakier than I expect, I begin moving into the cabin. Suddenly, there's a hand on mine.

"You're not going to walk down this aisle. Give me your boarding pass."

A woman with flaming-red hair and lots of freckles stands up. Her eyes are pleading and gentle.

"My seat is right here. 2A. Take it. I'll take yours," she says.

Before I can answer, she grabs my boarding pass and begins to collect her things: a laptop and a Louis Vuitton purse big enough for four small dogs. I look down at her ticket, which she has folded into my palm. Her name is Joni.

"Go ahead and sit down," she says.

Obediently, I settle in and watch her disappear into economy. As the world points and laughs, a hand on mine is a blessing.

I want to drink on the flight but don't. I just watch the perfectly spherical bubbles in my club soda break free from the sides of the cup and swim desperately for the surface, one after another, after another, and I pause occasionally to stare down through gaps in the clouds at the neat brown patches of earth that make up America's flyover country. I wonder if I'm a good person, something I have wondered frequently, almost obsessively, since childhood. I married Bruce for the right reasons, and I wanted to lead for the right reasons, but doing both successfully seemed to require a certain degree of transformation. Bruce loved my confidence, my toughness, and my dry wit, so I became all confidence, toughness, and dry wit. He was not allowed to see me weak or depleted, wanting or needing his help, wanting or needing his touch. Nashville loved that I was hopeful, courageous, and hip. With the help of the Machine, I distilled myself. I was nothing but hopeful, courageous, and hip. Give the people what they want. Get the vote. I've been trying to get the vote for as long as I can remember.

If you don't believe in yourself, nobody else will believe in you either.

Unless you're willing to lose yourself completely.

I lost myself. I wonder if the cost of a great leader is a good human. If it is, the cost is too great.

The plane lands late in Minneapolis with a lurch and shower of tentative applause. I don't see Joni with the red hair again, but the flight attendant tells me she's arranged transport to take me through the terminal to my next gate.

I'm the last to board my second flight to Bozeman, a two-and-a-half-hour hop over mostly soybeans and maize. There is no Joni this time. My temples throb, probably from wearing my sunglasses inside for the past six hours, as I walk to row fourteen, seat F. Out of necessity, I take my glasses off and shove them in my bag, trying not to make eye contact with anyone.

A mother and daughter are folded together and sobbing. They are carbon copies, small, birdlike blondes with faces that turn pink under duress. In this moment, they are shockingly pink. I heave my bag to the overhead bin as politely as possible and climb over them to the window, completing our neat little row of three. I don't say hello. I tell myself they're too exposed, too openly wounded to want company. I tell myself I wouldn't want somebody to say hello to me. While we taxi, I shut my eyes and try to disappear so that they can, but I'm listening. I have to.

They lost a husband and father sometime yesterday. It was sudden. Aunt Mary is calling the funeral home, the one near Second Street, not the religious one. Someone should call Roger. Roger would want to know. What about work? Someone should call work too. Whose name is the house in? I ache as they try to lose themselves in the arrangements, the clerical work of death. Inevitably, between bursts of thought, they return to their grief and just cry. Before I can understand, I'm crying too.

The plane takes off and the world once again becomes small. We cry over the heartland, accepting plastic cups of water and bags of impossibly tiny, twisted pretzels from the flight crew, who have no idea what else to do with us.

"It was a heart attack," the mother sobs to me. "He's just gone."

He's just gone.

Over the Dakotas, I lose Max again and again. His life comes at me, a fast-spinning carousel of baseball and friends and music and dogs, then, *that night*, pulling on my clothes, getting ready to offer condolences, finally realizing condolences were being offered to me.

He's just gone. Max was the one person who got all of me—my blood type, my smile, my laugh, my need to be what everyone wanted. He saw me ugly and sick and tired. He saw me fail when nobody else did. He saw me lose myself. He loved me. He *loves* me. As E and D weep, I reach out and grab their hands. It is my greatest, truest act of kindness.

"I'm so sorry. I lost my son last year. His name was Max."

• • •

For the next several days, my sister and I do "sister things" like yoga, walking in downtown Bozeman, and window-shopping on the main drag, a collection of Wild West–esque brick buildings that look as though they should be flanked by corrals instead of paid parking lots.

Heather doesn't press for too much information. She doesn't ask whether Bruce and I are going to stay together, which is good because I don't know. She doesn't ask what I'm going to do next, which is also good, because I have no idea. Her husband gives us a wide berth as he has probably been instructed to do. He can't be interfering with my soft landing, something Heather has choreographed carefully with clean towels, a visit to the nail salon, a series of Crock-Pot stews, and generous daily portions of fresh air and boxed wine.

In our family, Max and Bruce were always the outdoorsy ones. Traditionally, communing with nature is something I can take or leave. More often than not, I prefer the fat three-wick candle that smells like pine trees to the real stuff. Here, I feel differently.

Maybe it's because the gray squirrels and random jumping trout tend to not give a shit that I lost my son, my career, and possibly my marriage?

Maybe I have changed, or have always been like this but never known?

Maybe I just want to feel close to what I've lost—my son, my husband, my family?

Heather walks next to me, talking about her school, her students, the condition of the staff lounge. I half listen, looking up and round, trying to find the beginning and end of the giant blue heavens. What they say is true; it's a big fucking sky.

"How are you feeling?" Heather asks. It's the closest to a hard question she's asked since I arrived, and I don't know how to answer.

Counting the tops of the sugar pines and listening to their rustle, I feel Max's presence and absence in equal measure. I mourn the loss of his future and my own. I don't know what to do next. Heather stops to tie her shoe, and I lean against a sick tree that welcomes me with a shower of brittle needles. The fragrance travels deep, down to my toes, and I shed my labels—mayor, mom, ma'am. For a moment, I let myself be Megan again. What if that was always enough? What if I never needed to win? What if winning isn't what I thought it was?

I didn't come here to disappear. I came here to stop disappearing.

Heather looks up expectantly.

"I'm okay," I tell her. And I am okay. I'm not fabulous or clever or impressive. I'm okay. I'm average. I think, *I'm good.*

She smiles. I wonder how long she's been waiting for me to say that.

. . .

The headlines don't go on vacation when I do. Nashville is currently under the leadership of a new mayor who is nice, white, male, about the right age, and pleasant, like all the other mayors in America. The city audit continues. The prodding and tabulating and speculating continue, but I'm okay.

That night, after more brown food, I text Bruce.

> Let's talk when I get home.

No reply.

I'm surprised how badly I want to hear back from him. I don't know what comes next for us, but I hope it's something.

. . .

The Friday night before spring break ends, Heather wants to go out. I've forgotten that for my sister, this has been her vacation. No wonder she wants to do something before it ends besides watch my sorry-ass face.

"There's a great bar over in Manhattan that has a live band tonight and one of my friends does the vocals," she gushes. "It's called Exit 288 in honor of the Manhattan exit."

I try not to be too much of a snob. Small town, small bar, small band. How bad can it be? Perhaps it's a good way for me to dip my toes back into Nashville before putting my head under.

The room has a long bar with a tight dance space, created after stacking the Formica tables into a corner. There are a lot of regulars at the bar and Heather says hello to many of them. Nobody is dancing yet, but the band produces some pretty good ZZ Top and Thin Lizzie covers. Heather insists that it'll pick up later, but I'm hoping we'll be gone by then.

We sit at the bar, both of us poured into jeans that are a bit too tight, and I order a beer. You'd think with all the yoga and walking, I would be a couple of pounds lighter, but I've mopped up all that stew with big hunks of bread.

Heather goes to the bathroom. She says her underwear is stuck up her ass. Mine is too, but I stay put on my barstool.

The bartender is a woman, tatted with creatures on both arms but moving too quick for me to pick out a specific species from the collage of teeth, stripes, and tongues. She slides a Michelob Light my way and I thank her. She says, "No problem," fiddling with the television above the bar, changing the station repeatedly before settling on college basketball. She takes my Visa.

"Hey, my name is Megan," I tell her, taking a warm, bitter swallow of beer, "in case you need it for the tab."

She laughs, stops, and looks back at me. I can finally see a snake, a tiger, an owl, and a cat on her right bicep. It's a strange menagerie.

"I know who you are, darlin'," she says, grinning. "You're just one step ahead of the law, aren't ya?"

I look back, puzzled, and she goes on, "We get CNN here." And she goes back to stocking her fridge, amused.

If I can't hide in Manhattan, Montana, I can't hide anywhere. Most importantly, I don't want to. It's time to go home, not as the mayor, but as Megan, which I can already tell will be the much harder job.

Nesting

Nashville summer begins in April and leaves the city in a flushed, lightheaded stupor. The yard sprouts up in seven different shades of green. Squirrels stretch their long, gray bodies across the shingles to sunbathe on the roof outside the window of my home office, which I'm not sure can really be called an office anymore. It's just a room with an inkjet printer where I spend several hours a day staring at a blank screen, unsure at fifty-seven years old whether to draft a résumé, a tweet, or my last will and testament. The cursor just blinks, blinks, blinks. I blink back at it. I don't know what to do next, so I do nothing.

Outwardly, Bruce's life has not changed at all. While I'm sequestered in my inkjet printer room like a political Quasimodo, he does his Bruce things—teaching, riding his bike, reading his paper, walking his dogs. He has "no comment" on my resignation or the affair—not to me, Phil Williams, CNN, or Fox News, *never* to Fox News. The media wanted fireworks; he gave them doldrums, which I'm sure he found deeply satisfying. After about a week of watching him collect the recycling, pining for a glimpse of me disheveled, the paparazzi wandered off to greener, more salacious pastures. Bruce's only statement was a cryptic Groucho Marx quote on Twitter: "Learn from the mistakes of others. You can never live long enough to make them all yourself."

Even I don't understand exactly where he was going with it, and I can't ask. We're not there yet.

I pay attention to the last gasps of my administration's transit plan, and at the beginning of May, Nashville voters overwhelmingly reject it. It's not even close: 64 percent to 36 percent. It feels like the final salvo. I'm done. And I didn't even leave a legacy.

By June, most everyone has forgotten about what happened. The new mayor is doing fine. The Country Music Association Festival is coming up. Stormy Daniels, the porn star Trump allegedly had an affair with and paid off, is suing the president's fixer (I should've had a fixer). People have moved on from me, the blessing, I suppose, of a fast-moving news cycle. The only one who hasn't forgotten is Debby.

Debby from Ohio is still sending us her condolences each week, now addressing her cards "Mr. Bruce and Mrs. Megan Barry" instead of "Mr. Bruce and The Honorable Megan Barry." I feel a bit of a sting when I see it for the first time, but then again, I am no longer honorable and maybe never was.

I look forward to Debby days the way my dad looks forward to a new cookbook, knowing that he and Sig can spend the following days discussing recipes, planning dinner parties, and wondering which place settings will look best with which dish. While the topic isn't as interesting as a rising or falling political career, on Debby days, Bruce and I have something we can talk about with relative ease. Who is she? What's her motive? Does she have pets? The speculations are endless.

"Debby day!" I call out.

I'm standing in the kitchen with a wad of mail and a shimmering sky-blue envelope. It's the first Thursday of the month. On Thursdays, conditions seem especially ripe for a Debby card to arrive.

Bruce quickly dips in from the side porch to join me at the kitchen island, plucking the card from the clutches of a lawn care leaflet and stabbing through the seal with his thumb. He pulls out a small card, pale pink with a long-lashed fawn on the front. He opens it and a strange look crosses his face.

I watch him read. Something I've loved to do since we met.

"I think something's wrong with Debby," he says, handing the card to me.

He's right. The handwriting is shaky, and the return address has changed. We spend a few worried moments, wrapping our heads around the possibilities.

What's happening?

Did she have a stroke?

Is she dying?

We know nothing about Debby from Ohio but decided long ago that she must be a little disturbed. I mean, who sends cards over and over, week after week, to strangers? But truthfully, for the past eleven months, she's been the only thing bringing us back to each other, and to Max. I don't know what we'd do without her.

"What should we do?" I ask.

"I don't know," Bruce shrugs.

We look down with concern at the raggedy cursive, "Lovingly, Debby."

"Max would be so weirded out by this," I remark, staring down at the deer's plump, freckled backside (Debby loves a woodland theme). He would be as wrapped up in the mystery of the whole thing as we are, probably waiting for a severed thumb to arrive, tagged "Lovingly, Debby."

"Nah." Bruce smiles; it's a beautiful smile, with soft eyes and dimples. "Max would love Debby."

He's probably right. Max was a softy.

For an indeterminate length of time, however long it takes for sunset to become dusk, Bruce and I stand together deep in thought. I shut my eyes and try to remember Max's arms around me. I don't know if the love was unconditional, but the hugs were. And there can't be a lot of unconditional huggers on earth.

A few weeks later, on the one-year anniversary of Max's death, we receive our final letter from Debby, a crushing blow. She tells us she hopes her cards, all ninety-three of them, have been helpful. She chooses a family each year to receive them. This would be our last. There's no further explanation. We're on our own now.

"Celia Mae gave me the number of a couples therapist," I say as Bruce stares at the final woodland dispatch.

Bruce is not a therapy guy. I look back at him, waiting for the eye roll. It's instantaneous.

"Look, I know it's not your thing," I continue, "but we need to figure something out. I'm not happy. You're not happy."

He grumbles, indecipherably.

It would be an understatement to say that Bruce is skeptical of the rigors of the therapy certification process. Still, what we're doing on our own isn't working.

"Fine," he says. "Just let me know where to show up and when."

Our therapist is named Carol and she has an office on Music Row overlooking a one-way street people often forget is one-way (as evidenced by the frequent blasts of car horns and road rage).

The building is old, with a toilet that runs constantly and ant baits carefully positioned behind exactly the kind of floral waiting room furniture you would expect. It's our first appointment, so I get there early, before Bruce does, and leaf through a copy of *Real Simple* magazine. By the time I'm done leafing and Bruce has arrived, I'm wondering if a pantry makeover could actually fix everything that's wrong with us.

He walks in red-faced and puffing, unbuckles his bike helmet, and presses Carol's button on the index, illuminating it.

She pops out of the hallway a few seconds later, like a Sally Field jack-in-the-box.

"Hiiiiiii," she sings at us. "Why don't you come with me?"

Bruce looks at me like he can think of several reasons. I relish the fact that despite everything, he can still tell me a complete joke without saying a word.

The upstairs office is messy and brown like Bruce's, which seems to put him at ease. He's comfortable and is able, unlike me, to sit on the couch without scanning every title on her particle board bookshelf: *An Internal Family Systems Guide to Recovery from Eating Disorders*; *The Five Love Languages*; *His Needs, Her Needs*; *Eat, Pray, Love*; *The Ashram*.

Maybe we need to go to an ashram? I think, knowing that this room is as close to an ashram as Bruce Barry is ever going to get.

Carol sits in a futuristic-looking office chair and rolls slowly from side to side.

"So," she begins, "tell me what kind of work you're looking to do here."

"Probably the hard kind," I say back, hating myself for trying to be charming and witty.

Why do I always have to sparkle up?

She pity-laughs, and for the next half-hour she asks easy-to-answer questions.

"How long have you been married?"

"When did Max die?"

"When did the affair begin?"

Everybody, even the pros, wants the affair to be a Max thing.

"Have either of you thought of filing for divorce?"

Bruce is stoic when he relives it all, talking about Max and me like we're matters of scientific fact. I suppose in some ways we are. Max *is* gone. I *did* have sex with another man. This is accurate and pertinent information. As he speaks, unwaveringly, I wonder if I hurt him just to see if I still could.

When our fifty minutes are nearly up, Carol pulls out a big leather book and a pen and turns to face me, a ribbon of concern in the exact middle of her forehead.

"How would you like to move forward?" she asks.

I don't know. Together? Happily divorced? In an ashram?

"I'm not really sure," I tell her. "I don't know how to do this."

I'm crying a little. Her face softens.

"Well, how about we schedule out two weeks?" she suggests gently.

I'm the only one of us who didn't know she was talking about setting our next appointment. Bruce delights in the schadenfreude. He looks at me with what I'm almost sure is love.

• • •

Due to no fault of her own, we don't see Carol again. But Bruce and I make one decision that day. We decide to not get a divorce. It doesn't mean we're staying together—it just means we aren't hiring lawyers, dividing assets, and going our separate ways. Not yet, anyway.

Toward the end of summer, when the city is PBR-sweating through its Daisy Dukes, I rent an apartment in the Gulch, an area of town that used to be urban flotsam but is now boutique hotels and $25 parking. I realize how privileged this sounds in a place like Nashville, where a rent payment plus a mortgage payment for most people is not doable—but we dip into our modest savings to make it work. It's cheaper than getting a divorce and we need time apart. *Real* time. Bruce doesn't protest. I pack a suitcase and go, arriving in a space not unlike the one I revamped in the courthouse.

My mom buys me a new couch for my birthday, a velvety teal-blue beauty, with tufted pillows and modern lines, different than the over-stuffed, sagging, dog-hair covered, Pottery Barn–slipcovered number that takes up a tremendous amount of space in our family room at home, a relic from back in the days when I fancied us a Pottery Barn kind of family. I get a new bed and make the space livable, a place I want to spend time in and come back to, an apartment with a view of sky and clouds and sunrises and sunsets, not some shithole rent-by-the-week place like my dad had when he moved out when I was a kid—tacky; barely furnished, with plastic coverings on the couch that stuck to your thighs; rented to men who had been thrown out by their wives but still needed a place where the kids could come on the weekends. Not that kind of place. I try on for size what life will be like without—without being in my home, without being in my neighborhood, without being with someone I've spent twenty-five years with.

I don't talk to Bruce, or anyone really, for almost a month.

While I may have moved across town to escape my old life, my phone is still connected to several numbers in Hermitage, Tennessee, including a burner phone. I get a lot of hang-ups and pranksters, which comes with the territory.

By October, the No Caller ID calls have been popping up more frequently in my display. I usually hit Silence, but today I decide to answer.

"Hello?" I say, bracing for what I assume will be your run-of-the-mill expletive and hate-filled rant.

"Megan! Ooh good, I'm so glad I got you. I've missed you so much."

I say nothing and I wait.

"Megan, are you there? Megan?" the voice asks.

"I'm here," I say as the breath returns to my lungs. I remember to twinkle up and smile. Just to be an ass.

"It is so good to hear your voice. God, it's been so long. How are you?" he says.

"I'm fine, Rob. How are you?"

I've hardly thought about Rob. The fallout from the pictures, the federal proffer, the betrayal—these are all natural cues for him to fuck off into the sunset and never contact me again.

"I'm great," he replies. "The pension committee met today. It's all settled. I got my pension. I was so worried about that. They could have given me nothing, but they took off $1,000 because of the audit. Basically, I'm good. Thank God. I thought you would want to know."

The sunlight is streaming through my floor-to-ceiling windows in my apartment, and I can see the entire Nashville skyline at my feet.

"Say again?" I say, to be difficult. I have followed the news. I know the final hurdle for him was the pension meeting today to decide whether or not he gets his pension.

"I got my pension. I just thought you would be happy for me," he says giddily.

I am no Jesus, but right now I fantasize about Rob and Judas sharing a bunk. He was willing to sell me out for a price, a pension to be precise.

I'm not sure what I'm supposed to feel. The anger I felt is long gone, faded into ambivalence with an occasional dash of regret. I don't wish him ill. I don't wish him anything.

"Don't call me again," I say calmly and press the End button.

And I thought pressing the Megan Barry for mayor button in the voting booth was fun.

• • •

The last months of 2018 are filled with an array of stilted family get-togethers where nobody talks about what happened. We see Bruce's family around Thanksgiving, and we join my sister in Chicago for her annual Christmas party. After a single cranberry cosmopolitan, one of her friends asks me what I'm going to do next, and I tell him I don't know. After switching to gin, he tells me I shouldn't write a book. The festive season is survivable, but we don't do our regular things. There is no mid-December holiday blast with signature cocktails and catering and all our friends. There is no lighting of the Christmas tree downtown. There is still no Max.

Bruce is writing his columns again, something he couldn't do while I was in office. Often, I wonder what kind of story he would have written about me if I was just another immoral politician and not his wife. I expect it would be biting, brutal, and very funny. I probably would have laughed at it—if it wasn't about me.

It's funny how you can be so proud of yourself one day and so ashamed the next.

• • •

Bruce reaches out on a Thursday. It's the beginning of January, and though I haven't lived at home in five months, Bruce and I have been talking. When he does write something, he shares it with me. When I need to figure out where to position *felon* on my résumé, I call him.

"Hi, Meggie," he says.

Nobody else calls me Meggie. Just when I think I'm ready to start dividing assets, unfailingly, he'll hit me with a "Meggie."

"My schedule this semester is a bit of a mess. Especially Tuesday/ Thursday. Do you think you could swing by and let the dogs out once in a while? I can get Bonnie to do it if you can't."

Bonnie lives in a rental down the street and is somewhere between the ages of sixty and seventy. She subsists on a small Social Security check padded, albeit not luxuriously, with income from helping us with errands and housekeeping. Her specialty is laundry, but I'm sure she'd be open to dogs if I don't want to do it, but my schedule is clear. I spend most of my time staring out the windows at the towering cranes in my new neighborhood and telling myself how this used to be my town. Tuesdays and Thursdays are wide open.

"I'd love to!" I tell him.

"You're sure?" he asks.

"Totally sure," I promise. "I really miss the pups."

And I do really miss them, along with my favorite coffee mug, the squirrels on the roof, the groan of the floorboards, and Bruce.

It's settled. He says he'll leave me a key, and I remind him that I still have one. Home is still home. I just haven't seen it in a while.

As promised, the following Tuesday I slide my key into the lock and hear the perfect duo of thwacking tails and muffled half-barks, along with the refrigerator chugging along. Hank throws himself at me when I cross the threshold and bug-eyed Boris is frozen with joy. It smells like mildew and dirty dishes.

I walk to the kitchen and open the side door. The dogs bound into the yard with a shocking lack of coordination. I look around and take everything in, sights and smells. The (former) mayor's office has been moved into the sunroom and is spilling into the dining room. A stack of boxes towers from floor to ceiling next to several rolled-up rugs, a chair, and some mementos. Bruce hasn't touched any of it. Junk mail covers the table I used as a desk and the actual dining table where my political career was born and buried. The chair I used to sit in while he talked to me about American foreign policy or the Mets or John Lennon or whatever he was fascinated with that day holds a backlog of *New Yorker*s and the new Murakami book.

Objectively, the place is a mess and, it seems, so is Bruce. All he has in the refrigerator is ketchup, an open bottle of wine, and four slices of expired ham.

I'm contemplating a swig of the wine when something skates by on the floor. Another something skates after it.

Mice. Fucking mice.

Hank appears at the side door whimpering. Boris stands behind him trembling. While the two are brilliant at scaring our neighbors, the local vermin are unphased.

I investigate the corners of the kitchen, and behind a bookshelf I find a telltale nest of tissue, paper, and hair. Seedlike turds line the cupboards and backs of the wine racks. I follow the turds to what appears to be a well-traveled route from the kitchen to the dog food.

"Jesus Christ," I say to the mice. "This is some real investment in transit."

I text Bruce:

> We've got a problem. Going to Home Depot.
> Staying over.

He replies:

> Okay. Sounds good.

That afternoon, I buy several different varieties of mouse bait, Lysol wipes, and some new ham, sliced thin. Somewhere between the deli counter and the self-checkout, I realize that I still love my husband. The love is a relief, from the shame, the guilt, the regret.

Bruce and I spend an entire weekend together cleaning up mouse shit and setting traps. By the end, I know I want to come home.

Sin, Forgiveness, Crazy, Grief

A young man who looks like Max is standing beside me. We're at Café Lula, a bar next to the Ryman Auditorium. Bruce and I always stop here to have a drink before a show, which today is a '70s swamp rock band we both love that has almost none of its original members. Because everyone sounds like God at the Ryman, it'll be fantastic.

The kid has long, dark hair that curls at the ends and the earnest beginnings of a beard that, bless it, will probably go nowhere. His baseball hat is turned backward, with the plastic band across his forehead, leaving a bright-pink mark on his skin. It's the exact same way Max wore his hat.

"Who does he remind you of?" I ask Bruce, who is deep in the observation of other people, currently a small group of girls who are actively embarrassed by the bachelorette party they've thrown, drinking shyly out of penis-shaped straws and realizing that this bar is the wrong kind of bar for plastic tiaras and dick necklaces.

I poke him in the ribs and nod to my left toward not-Max.

"Who do you see?" I whisper, but loudly.

"Really?" he says. "You have to ask?"

He goes back to his wine, mildly irritated that I interrupted his people watching. I continue trying to force eye contact with the person who is not my son but could be from a distance. He has the wrong kind of eyes, but he smells a bit like weed and Mennen deodorant, which cancels out the wrong kind of eyes every time.

Bruce and I are somewhere between reconciliation and resignation. I never stopped wearing my ring, except on a few occasions in bed when I wanted to know what it might feel like. So many years of ring wearing had warped my finger to look small and girdled in the middle. After we caught and released the many mice living at our home, we started to get together more often, a movie on the weekend or dinner or a drink on the porch. We both wear readers. Being together is easier than texting each other in evening light.

Not-Max abandons his post next to me at the bar to join a table of his friends, and I feel the loss all over again. I watch him travel across the room in his boat-sized shoes, holding a Modelo Negra that looks small in his hand. A girl with green hair and a dice tattoo stands up to greet him. He hugs her, and I want these to be scenes from Max's life so badly that I could cry. I do cry.

"Pass me a napkin," I tell Bruce. "Quick."

My eyes are welling at an alarming rate. I have to tilt my head back so I don't ruin my makeup or cause a scene. Bruce looks embarrassed but hands me a cocktail napkin anyway.

"Meggie, it's not him," Bruce says, trying to be a little tender and shaking his head. "You need to stop. I'm going for a smoke."

He grabs his coat and I watch him exit onto the expanse of the patio, hunching his shoulders, looking cold and distant through the glass. *Why can't you just let me have this?* We've talked about everything the past month except the things we need to talk about—Max and our marriage.

Bruce is always online in time to secure great seats, and tonight, we are front-row balcony, to the side. Below us, an usher is seating not-Max in a crowded row on the floor. I can look down on him easily but try not to do it too often. I don't want to creep out the poor kid and I don't want to bother Bruce, who is bothered but will never say so, let alone reveal why.

Maybe I embarrass him? Though crying in public seems tame compared to the shit I've already pulled. Maybe it's the shit I've pulled? "Isn't that the old mayor who had sex with her bodyguard?" "Wow, he actually stuck around," and "What is she going to do now?" are just a few of the whispers we've picked up over the course of the evening. This is the sort of thing that would've been perfect to bring to Carol.

After an hour of what sounds to me like the same guitar riff, I tell B I'm going for more wine. He's transfixed. This is his happy place, an old building filled with rock and roll and the musty smell of a thousand shows. I head up the aisle through clusters of dancing people, dodging the swaying and smiling bodies and trying not to jostle anyone's beer. I'm almost to the bar when I feel my body spring into and off something. I look up. It's not-Max. He barely feels the impact.

"Hey! You were standing next to me at the bar before the show," I exclaim.

My pulse is wild. He seems kind of buzzed and doesn't seem totally sure where he's going.

"Yeah," he says with a nod, "I think so."

His grin is like a yawn, slow and comfortable. I spot a chipped tooth, a chipped tooth that Max didn't have. I try to unsee it.

"You look like someone I used to know," I tell him.

He looks immediately uncomfortable. "Yeah . . . cool."

I try to grab his attention, my voice drops, and I look straight into his wrong-colored eyes, trying to steal them from the dancing spotlights. "You look like my son."

"My name is Megan," I tell him, holding out my hand. Confused, he accepts it but while taking a step back.

"I'm Brian," he says.

I want to reach out and hug him. He knows that I want to and it's awkward. It can't be any other way.

His wrong eyes shift back and forth, and I finally snap out of it.

His name is Brian. Not Max.

But I so want him to be Max. I so want Max to be sitting at the Ryman with a green-haired girl, flush faced, ecstatic, and two beers in.

"Nice to meet you, Brian." I pat his arm and join the line, not looking back. When I return to my seat, we sway to the music of Little Feat. I think about Dallas Alice and Lowell George and another overdose. I'm crying again, but Bruce doesn't seem to notice. It's okay because there are plenty of things I'm avoiding too.

I'm waiting for Bruce to say, "I love you. Come home." He's already told me he forgives me. I fantasize about him saying things while I'm up in my concrete tower (which we increasingly can't afford). Even if Bruce forgives me, even if Nashville forgives me, it doesn't mean I'll forgive myself.

* * *

I'm at the house on a Thursday letting Boris and Hank out when I hear Bonnie come in to do her errands. I think she has her own key now. Or maybe she just knows where the secret key is. Most of Nashville knows where the secret key is because one of the stations filmed me retrieving it. You would think they would know better than to play it on national television.

"Bonnie? Is that you? I'm here today," I say so I won't startle her. I join her at the bottom of the stairs. Wordlessly she walks into the kitchen and washes the three dishes in the sink. If there are teams, Bonnie is Team Bruce.

She weighs less than one hundred pounds soaking wet and her skinny white arms remind me of aspen branches. She's had cancer somewhat recently, but her latest CAT scan is clean. She's very proud of it, though she still smells a little like the unfiltered cigarettes she claims to not smoke anymore. We're all caught up on laundry and Boris just took a dump in the azaleas. I have a different job for us today.

"We've got something bigger than laundry today," I tell her, "if you're interested."

Max's old room is filled with boxes labeled "correspondence." I found them while I was dealing with the mice. While I was in office, I received thousands of cards, random letters, and gifts in the mail, some sent to my mayor address and others sent here. It isn't too challenging to dig up the address of a public figure online these days. It's so easy, even Fox News can do it.

After a few death threats, a pair of stripper boots, and some fairly graphic nudes, I stopped opening the mail and left it to Elease, who brought me a curated collection of not-creepy, well wishes every week. When the affair broke, her mail deliveries stopped (I'm guessing things took a turn then), but she saved all of the correspondence in several boxes. I feel compelled to go through it all before I toss it.

"Been wondering about these," she says, rolling up the sleeves of her too-large sweatshirt and looking at the boxes, a sheen of scalp showing through her white hair. She seems intrigued, intrigued enough that she might be willing to skip her afternoon serving of Judge Mathis to help me sort through these.

"Look, I don't know what's in these letters," I warn her. "It could be anything . . ."

"I've seen letters," Bonnie says, quick enough to make me believe that she has, in fact, seen all kinds of letters.

"We'll go and do some piles," she decides (this is Bonnie's preferred method of organization). I'm way ahead of her. After working with her, I know that "some piles" is the best method of organization for anything. I've decided on three dominant categories: sin, forgiveness, and crazy. I already have a whole closet full of boxes marked "grief."

At first, it's pretty easy. Bonnie folds her small, rakish body into a cross-legged position and zealously begins unsealing envelopes and talking. Bonnie likes helping us, but what she really likes is to talk. She wants to tell me about the other renters in her house. She wants to tell me that one of said renters passed away recently and she could smell him. For days. She wants to tell me that her landlord wouldn't authorize her to go into the apartment to check on him.

"I knew he was dead," she says.

She wants to describe in detail how the body lay half on and half off the bed and how when they finally did go in, he was so swollen and decomposed, he was hardly recognizable.

"And now, we have to replace the whole floor because he went and seeped into it." She shakes her head.

I remind her that he didn't go and do anything, which she finds funny.

"I suppose you're right," she laughs.

I'm glad she's talking. People write strange things to people they don't know. I don't want to think about it too much.

The sin letters go in lots of different directions, but the main road is accusatory: husbands blaming me for their wives' affairs, wives blaming me for making other wives look bad. Our favorite begins with "You done did to your husband what my wife done did to me." Several Bible verses later, the gentleman asks me if I want a date and includes a picture. Not my type.

The forgiveness and grief letters are sad and sweet. They usually include personal stories about loss, mistakes the writer has made, and recovery stories. Some seek absolution. One includes a $25 gift certificate to Golden Corral so Bruce and I can have a date night. Some just want me to know I'm not alone. Some just say, "I'm sorry," two powerful, earth-moving words. The crazy letters are either totally nonsensical or sinister.

"Which category do you think this one will fall into—crazy, sin, or forgiveness?" I ask, holding up a white envelope with a typed label taped to the front.

"Definitely crazy," Bonnie says.

The postmark reveals nothing except that it was mailed in Nashville a few days ago. I've received several that look just like it at home since we went public with the affair.

I slice it open and take out the single white sheet of paper. It's another one from Max. From the grave.

Mommy,

I have now transitioned over, and I am waiting for you to join me in HELL. Where we can spend eternity together, this is where we belong, Mommy!

Do not view my death as a tragedy, it was not, it was a choice. Come join me soon. Waiting on you in HELL.

XOXO
Max

Bonnie grabs it.

"That's just sick," she says.

"Yeah, it's pretty twisted. Let me get one of the others and we can compare."

I have a whole stack of ones in the crazy pile. They all have the same type of envelope and the same typed address label affixed with tape; many also include pictures of me with handwritten comments. Remarks about blow jobs and how fat I am.

I pull out one that seems similar. I had received it close to the one-year anniversary of Max's death.

"This one looks the same." I group them in the same pile and set them aside.

"Who sends this kind of sick shit?" Bonnie shrieks.

I have my suspicions, but it could be anyone. I lit a lot of people's lives on fire and broadcast it on national television. They all get to be angry at me for the rest of their lives.

"I hope you call the cops and they find that son of a bitch who sent that! Hope they pay!"

My guess is that they already have.

Bonnie goes home around 4 PM, leaving me in what now seems like a large and lonely room. We've sorted and stored all the letters. The only thing worse than a monument to my failed career in my son's old bedroom is nothing at all, the feeling that I've crossed a bridge from infamy to insignificance. Aside from "Max," no one is writing anymore. Not even Debby.

• • •

It's cold. I pull into the grocery store parking lot and get out of the car. The early-spring air smells like Krispy Kreme donuts and wet pavement. I pull my jacket tight and walk past a beautiful old truck—the kind you see in country music videos. Beside it, there's a Volkswagen Golf slapped with a pristine bumper sticker that says, "Dance like No One's Watching."

Newsflash. Somebody's always fucking watching.

216

The window of the truck is down, so I nod and say hey to the driver. She looks out her side window.

"It's you," she says.

"Yep, it's me." I smile.

I can usually tell by the tone which direction we're headed, but today my guard is down. I'm just here for dog food and bread.

"Have you set yourself right with Jesus and God?" the woman demands.

Her eyes narrow and she tilts her head just slightly to the left, like I better not give her any more bullshit. Familiar territory.

"Yep, all good. God and Jesus and me—we're like this." I press my palms together in a prayer. "But I appreciate you asking."

I'm not being flip or condescending. I *am* good with God and Jesus, albeit not many others. I give her a wave and keep walking.

"Wait," she says. "I have another question. It's about the woman, the woman whose husband you cheated with? Did you ever apologize to her?"

You've gotta be fucking kidding me.

I take a step back and look more closely at her face. *My* eyes narrow. Do I know her? She looks like a thousand other women my age— blonde hair streaked with darker roots and workout clothes—nope, I don't know her.

I smile again, but my lips are tight, my teeth are hidden, and my cheeks go up only enough to make it look like I'm not grimacing. My team always said it was my annoyed smile. Not very twinkly.

"Have a good day," I tell her and walk into the store. I'm shaken.

It hadn't occurred to me to apologize to Sheri. Sure, I'm responsible for what has probably been and will remain the worst year of her adult life, but I can't imagine she'd want to grab a martini and gab about it. I'm sure she knows I'm sorry. I said it on television.

But what if she doesn't?

Or what if she doesn't believe it?

I dart down aisle five like I'm being chased, then aisle three, grabbing the Purina and Nature's Own whole wheat and blazing through the self-checkout. Nobody recognizes me. As soon as I get back to the car, I pick up the phone and call my mother. She picks up on the first ring like always.

"Mom, do you have a couple of minutes? I need to ask you something." I speak quickly. Besides, this feels urgent. She knows something's up.

"Sure. What's going on?" she asks.

"Would it have mattered if any of the people Dad cheated with apologized to you? I mean, it's not like they're responsible for Dad's actions. *He* was the cheater. *He* was the one married to you. He was the one who . . ." I stop myself before she can.

Mom also isn't one for rambling.

"Yes, Megan," she says with a sigh. "Actually, yes, it would have. When you do something wrong, you apologize."

I pull out of the lot and head home, passing "Dance like No One's Watching" one more time.

Later that night, I write my own letter in my own handwriting with my return address. I mail it to Sheri. I was selfish. I was cruel. I am sorry for all the pain I caused her and her family. She did nothing to deserve this.

Second Act

I scan the parking lot of the no-tell motel for a late-model truck. The motor-court motto "Where the Stars Stay" is written in lights to reel people in off the interstate. There's a parking space in front of each room and a swimming pool smack in the middle.

At least it's not shaped like a fucking guitar, I think to myself.

I've been told that I need to try room 251 first. Will's mom isn't sure, but she thought she heard him say something about 251. It's right in the middle of the block. I knock.

Nothing.

I knock again and then gently push on the door. It isn't even shut. The only thing that keeps it from flying open is the thickness of the dirty beige carpet on the inside.

"Hello?" I call out. "Helloooo!"

I sound like somebody's mother, but I am somebody's mother. And I'm looking for somebody's son.

The room is in disarray, towels draped over the skinny beds, sheets crumpled at the end of the mattresses, revealing thick plastic sheaths. There are two large black garbage bags with clothes spilling out on the floor. A young man, whose pupils are barely pinpricks, comes out of the bathroom. His hair is still wet. He looks to be in his midtwenties and is clean-shaven and a little heavyset. He's wearing a long-sleeved black button-down even though it's eighty-five degrees outside. The only people who dress like that are addicts and maître d's. He seems to be in a hurry.

"Hey!" he says with a grin.

He's amiable and very high. High enough that he's not at all surprised to see me, a stranger, within six inches of his dirty underwear.

"Do you know where Will is?" I ask.

"He was here a minute ago. You *just* missed him. I'm sure he'll be right back," he assures me. Quickly, he scans the room to make sure there's nothing I can see that he doesn't want me to.

"Are you sure I just missed him?" I press. "I've been in the parking lot for a while. I didn't see anyone leave."

"Oh yeah, I'm sure," he says. "I think he was hungry and went to get some food."

Will was one of Max's friends. His mom is out of town and called this morning to ask if I could help find him. She and his dad don't know where he is or what he's using these days. It used to be pills, but when everyone caught onto the pills, it became heroin, which is cheaper and easier to find. He has his dad's truck, but there are seven trucks here that all look roughly the same. He shouldn't be driving. Making sure he doesn't hurt anyone else is about as much as his family can do right now. Protecting him from himself, I know, is a different matter entirely.

The guy starts to look more nervous, picking at the buttons on his shirt and straightening the room a little. When I arrived, it seemed as though he was going somewhere, but now he appears to be in no hurry.

"Who are you, and how do you know Will?" I ask.

He swallows. His Adam's apple is enormous.

"I'm his roommate. We met in rehab. We're both doing really great."

Lies. I see right through him.

"Sure, you are. Good for you. What's your name? Where are you from? Where's Will?" I demand.

He's scared. I'm scaring him. He clears his throat and licks his lips. He's picking at his nails.

"I'm from around, you know, just staying here until I can find a job and then get an apartment and . . ."

He's talking fast and I've noticed he's started shoving all the clothes in the room into the trash bags.

"Those are Will's clothes. Is he here?" I ask. It's a gamble. I have no idea what Will's clothes look like.

"Will? I don't think so. It's just me in here." A nervous laugh shudders through his body. I realize I'm not going to get any real information out of him, so I step back outside and scan the parking lot.

Will's mom texts:

> Anything?

I respond:

> Not yet. What kind of truck am I looking for again?
> What's the license plate?

She replies instantaneously. I'm looking for a black Dodge Ram with Texas plates.

I begin to make my way around the horseshoe of cars and spot it quickly. The back bumper looks like it's been in a recent accident. The driver's door is ajar, and a white Converse sneaker is poking out, just barely.

Shit.

I go numb and start running.

"Will!!!" I yell.

It's a miracle I don't yell, "Max!" Inside, I am screaming for him.

"Will! Come on!"

I fling the door open. Will is slumped over the wheel. The truck is idling. I reach across and pull the keys from the ignition. His body is totally limp. The only thing holding him in the truck is his seat belt. Dark foam escapes from the corners of his mouth. It's viscous and russet brown. I grab for his wrist to feel his pulse but suddenly forget how to find it and everything else I'm supposed to do in this situation. I look down and realize I'm just holding his hand.

Shit.

Is he overdosing?

Where's my Narcan?

Where's my phone?

"Will!" I shake him, violently, remembering the careful way he lifted his pizza slice from a box in our kitchen, the color in his cheeks, that he used to call me "Miss Megan," that he knew to place his dishes in the sink and say, "Thank you for having me."

His eyes roll back a little and he grunts. He's alive.

He opens his eyes. "Megan? What are you doing here?"

Okay. He's talking.

I dial 911. "Possible overdose," I spit into the phone and give the address.

The fire truck arrives in seconds, and at the same time a large, tattooed man pulls into the space next to us.

"I'm here to take Will. Who are you?" he says. He has a deep voice, like Papa Bear or the great and powerful Oz.

"Will's mom sent me," I reply. "I'm Megan."

"She sent me too. I'm supposed to pick him up and take him back to rehab. I'm Steve," he says, his tone softening. We're on the same team.

The EMTs want to examine Will. Carefully, they lift him out of the truck and prop him against the driver-side door. I notice the bag of chocolate chip cookies at his feet and watch him wipe away the black goo from his mouth. The innocence is crushing. The boy smoked heroin and bought cookies.

"I'm fine, Megan," Will mumbles. "I'll go with Steve."

The EMTs give him the okay and he hops into the back of Steve's car, and just as suddenly as Steve appeared, he and Will are gone.

I walk back to my car and text his mom.

> Steve came and got him. I hope Steve is real. I hope he really meant it when he said he was taking Will back to rehab.

Steve works there, it turns out.

I put Will's keys in my purse and head home. About a mile down the road, I catch a glimpse of Will's roommate, walking at a good clip away from the motel and glancing over his shoulder. He's carrying the trash bags and sweating through his shirt. He is somebody's son too.

* * *

If I were looking for parenting advice, a disgraced local politician who lost her son to an overdose probably wouldn't be my first call. Even before my life imploded in real time on NewsChannel 5, I didn't exactly smack of wisdom for the ages, but people have started coming to me for help. Friends, *their* friends, strangers, anyone trying to support someone with substance use disorder. For all my faults, I'm easy enough to talk to. I can listen, and mostly that's all I do. There's an inexplicable closeness people feel, I guess, when they've watched you unravel in a spectacular and public way. Whatever dark place they're in, they can feel confident that I've already been there, gotten the passport stamp, and been made an honorary citizen. It's a way to serve with no spin, no twinkling up, and no endgame, which is probably the way service is meant to be.

The day before Max died, he called me concerned about his friend Wyatt. I was at the office when Max's photo appeared on my screen. Max and I were texters. A call, at least a call on purpose, meant something serious.

"Momma," he said, "Wyatt's in trouble."

He confessed to me that his friend Wyatt had been using, and he wondered if it was time to call his mom. So we did. Right then. I listened as he told her Wyatt needed help. She cried and thanked us.

Max felt better. I was so proud.

Still ferociously type A and trying to make Max's every move into a respectable vocation, I thought, *Maybe it's this? Maybe this is the work Max is meant to do here?*

And it might have been. But now, it's my work. I can't bring my son back, but I can carry him forward.

· · ·

In May, I offer myself up to any organization that will have me. Never have so many nonprofit CEOs raised their eyebrows at about the same time. It's not like I resigned yesterday, but I'm not radiating spokesmom energy either. They do like that I'm willing to work for free and that I'm available. So available. Slowly, opportunities arrive to share Max's story and mine, stories that I realize as time passes are woven together by more than the stuff of mothers and sons. Our stories are about shame and forgiveness. Our stories are about the toll of pretending to be something you're not to become someone who matters. Our stories are about losing yourself. Mine, by the grace of God, is about having the humility to try to find yourself all over again, in a world that has already made its judgments and cast its votes. But my vote matters too. I respect myself. I'm proud of myself. I'm not the most important person in the room, but now I know I never needed to be.

I don't miss the office furniture I couldn't really afford, the photo ops with Hillary Clinton, the endless exposure to fundraiser cheese boards, the Calvin Klein shift dresses, and boundless ambition. I really don't miss the Spanx. I miss the things I couldn't see when I had all of that at my fingertips. I miss Max. Max, the unconditional hugger, terrible baseball player, and dog person. Max, who never cared if a person was great just as long as they were good. Max, who I feel with me as I walk, held in the shade of shaggy willows and towering elms at the cemetery off Fourth Avenue, a place where gray squirrels frisk and people come for the quiet. We interred him there on the one-year anniversary of his death. I am still so proud of him. He was good, and I know a little bit more now about how hard it is to be good in this world. I try every day to be a little less ambitious, a little less important, and a little more good.

● ● ●

Somewhere in the summer of 2020, we decide it makes sense to get the apartment off the monthly bills. I come home with my blue couch. For once, the dogs are most excited to see me. Our marriage is mostly what it was: banter, dogs, companionship, and morning coffee. There are things we should talk about, but don't. There are moments when I want to be held and I'm not. But I love Bruce.

I love him because he gives Boris ham.

I love him because he makes me laugh.

I love him because he likes to sit on the porch and just talk.

I love him because he's the smartest person I know.

I love him because he researches everything.

I love him because he loves Colorado.

I love him because he is Max H Barry's dad.

• • •

It's December 8, 2020, the anniversary of John Lennon's death, and we're making enchiladas. Bruce's face is turned into the last of the afternoon sun, obscuring his features. I can't read what he's thinking, but I've never really been able to. A marriage is funny that way. We never know each other entirely; we get used to the things we don't know.

Bruce's dimples are more pronounced when he shuts his mouth and turns it upward. He never has a full-toothed smile; he closes his lips and looks mildly amused. I look once, see the dimples, and continue grating cheese. I look again and notice that he's crying.

"I miss him so much, Meggie," he says. He reaches for his phone and opens the app for our music. "Don't hate me for what I'm going to play. I know it's going to make you sad."

I'm chopping onions, so I'm a goner anyway.

"I remember exactly where I was the day John Lennon died. I was twenty-three and working on my master's thesis. They let me have access to the typewriter at night, and I was listening to the radio. They started playing all Lennon songs. I knew something bad must have happened to him," he says.

I stir the ground chicken, breaking it up with my spatula, a spatula that always bends and I hate.

Bruce's Lennon playlist pours through the Sonos. He's crooning "Bring It on Home to Me," a bluesy Sam Cooke cover that I haven't heard before.

"This isn't making me sad," I say softly. I'm missing something. Bruce never cries.

I take the food processor from the drawer and place it on the cabinet, watching him. I add spinach, salsa, peppers, and onions and push Pulse, still watching him.

"I think some of my happiest memories are the times Max and I spent together in Tacoma," he remembers. "We would just get in the Honda CR-V and drive around. I remember being out there one time and having to take the car to a carwash. He'd broken a window and hadn't cleaned out all the glass shards. There were still some in the backseat."

We're not talking about John Lennon anymore.

"And then there were all those times we drove out together to Colorado. We would choose a couple of books on tape. I would let him choose the music. We really bonded over some of that stuff I never would have listened to if he hadn't made me. All that '90s rap." He sniffs.

Bruce's shoulders start to shake. I suddenly have the feeling of not knowing what to do with my hands. I take the cauliflower tortillas out of the freezer and heat up another pan on the stove. I need to thaw them and make them a little crispy.

"Nobody Told Me" is up next, from Yoko and John's final album.

I grab some zucchini and decide to add those too. The cutting board slides around on the counter as I take the dull knife and slice through the skin.

B looks up. "I promise I'll sharpen those this weekend."

He glances back to the phone, and soon "Imagine" fills the room. He jacks up the volume. We look at each other and sing the first verse together. His cheeks are red and his eyes well again.

I grab the Pyrex pan to start assembling the enchiladas. A row of the green chicken sauce, then zucchini, more sauce, quartered tortillas, a sprinkling of the cheese, repeat. I spray the aluminum foil with Pam and wrap it tightly around the dish.

"It's sad he died so young. So senseless." I put dinner in the oven.

Tentative and not wanting to intrude, I reach for my wine glass and join Bruce around the other side of the counter. He looks at me as "Beautiful Boy" begins to play.

"I miss Max so much, Meggie," he says, completely undone, tears flowing freely, body shaking.

Now, I'm crying. *We* are crying.

I hold him and he doesn't pull away.

The sun begins to dip behind the trees out the window, a horizon that has remained unchanged as so much else has shifted shape. I can see his face again. The tears are dry now and our bodies part. He looks older and sadder than I expect. I'm older and sadder too.

He steps back toward me, and for a moment his hand finds my back. We don't look at each other. Instead, our eyes fall to the melting orange sun.

"I didn't know how to fix it, Bruce. I'm so sorry," I tell him.

"I know you are."

There's a weightlessness to the moment, the feeling that we're enveloped in sky rather than staring out at it behind smudged panes of glass. There's a feeling of love.

And in this moment, I know exactly what to do next. I wrap my arms around my husband and my touch doesn't make him bristle or squirm. His dimples appear again, and he hugs me back.

Mayor, Nashville, Tennessee

Mayoral Election, Nashville, Tennessee, 2015

Megan Barry: 60,519 votes

David Fox: 49,694 votes

Time is dripping slowly, in small jewels I want to trap in the palm of my hand, hold gently, and study closely, savoring each second as it unfolds. I want to remember everything, every sip of drink and breath of air, every face in the room, an ocean of skin and eyes and lips and ears that blend together, forming an impossible thing of beauty. This is my home. *My* city.

I step onto the stage. It's almost time to begin. In a wave of white light from the back of the house, the world blurs. The sea of faces becomes shadow, sitting calmly beneath the brightness. My term hasn't even started yet, and already I never want it to end.

Jason Isbell and Amanda Shires finish up "Something More Than Free" and pop their instruments into their cases, walking off to watch from the wings. Even without their strumming, this afternoon is an endless piece of music, all the songs accompanied by the din of joyous laughter and rain on the roof.

"Are you ready?" Bruce says.

"I am," I tell him. "You?"

A voice I know but can't name calls me. It's time to take my oath.

We approach the lectern together, as a family, Max, dressed in his charcoal suit jacket, walking one step ahead of me, and Bruce, walking one step behind. His hand finds my shoulder to linger softly for just a minute, a forgettable gesture to anyone but me. Here, now, in a moment too big for me to understand, that hand is a beacon. *I'm still here*, it says. *I will always be here.*

We stop, center stage, and wait for Judge Dinkins to begin.

Max looks down at his shoes, probably to avoid the heat of the bulbs and, maybe, the eyes of the two thousand people in front of him. His hair is pulled back in a ponytail, a compromise between him and my team, who would have preferred he cut it short and style it neatly. I'm glad that he didn't. This is Max, my Max, the most important person in the room. Cocooned by ambient sound, held in the light, it's just the three of us. Maybe I'll be happier one day, but I doubt it. This is everything I've ever wanted.

Judge Dinkins starts talking. His voice is sweet and low, and we know it well. He was Max's baseball and basketball coach. He flicked stray gravel from Max's scraped knees, bolstered his broken confidence, tore open his Popsicles, and called him on his shit. Judge Dinkins has loved us for nearly twenty years. We love him back.

I raise my right hand and start repeating after the judge. I make promises. I make them with my whole heart, Max and Bruce, standing by as my witnesses. There are the promises I say out loud and the ones I keep to myself. I promise to be good and stay good. I promise to give this my everything. I promise to remember why I'm here. I promise to remember who I am and who I'm here with today. There are other witnesses beneath the lights, but these two are mine, always.

It's over suddenly, sooner than I expect. Applause shatters through the room. People are hooting and joyous. The lights shift and brighten. There are thousands of faces, and still somehow it's just Bruce, Max, and me. Bruce's hand finds my shoulder again, making a series of un-Bruce-like pats. Max wraps me up in his arms, dulling the rest of the world the way only his embrace can. He pushes his glasses up his nose and swipes at the wetness in the corners of his eyes. I wonder how many tears he's had that he's never let fall. I'm not sure how long we hold each other, but it's never long enough.

"I'm so proud of you, Momma," he says softly. In the peace and quiet of each other, in the noisiest world I've ever known, it dawns on both of us, *I won.*

ACKNOWLEDGMENTS

Stories like this don't get told unless a lot of people insist that they do. I want to thank the incredible humans who showed up and kept showing up when I was living this story and throughout the process of writing and publishing it.

Bruce, I know I said there were no heroes and no villains in this story, but I lied—you're the hero. Thank you for loving me all the way to hell and back.

Max, you taught me everything I know about love and grace, and you continue to teach me. I see you in rabbits and squirrels and smiles and long-haired kids and fishing rods and hip-hop and the state of Colorado. Thank you for being everywhere. I love you. Being your mother and carrying your legacy is the greatest gift and honor of my life.

To my family, my mom, Jan, my dad, Ken and Sig, my sisters, Heather and Kristin and Molly. I love you all so much. Thank you for believing in me then, now, and always. Dad, the world is ready for your memoir now.

To Bruce's family, you took your cues from Bruce and kept loving me and including me even when you were unsure what the next steps should be. Thank you.

Margaret Riley King and Sophie Cudd, the most unstoppable agenting team on earth, you fought tooth and nail for me and this story, and I am beyond grateful to you both.

Shannon Lee Miller, this never would have happened without you. Thank you for loving every part of this story and helping me bring it to life. It's your turn now to write your own story. I can't wait to read it.

Matt Holt, Katie Dickman, Lydia Choi, Jennifer Brett Greenstein, Jessika Rieck, and all the wonderful (and patient) copy editors and proofreaders at BenBella and Matt Holt Books, there's no place like home—thank you for giving me and this book such a great one.

To my PR and social media teams, Mallory Hyde and Kerri Stebbins, Savannah Prine, and Lauren Loisel, you are champions and I love you. It isn't always easy to promote a book that gently suggests we dismantle the patriarchy in a still-patriarchal world.

To all the amazing people—my team, who helped me win the mayor's race and then helped me govern—my deepest sadness still is the interruption I caused in your lives because of my mistakes. Please know how grateful I still am for everything you did and have continued to do and how much I love and respect you. I am still humbled by the love you showed me when I was at my best and my worst. Thank you. We are Nashville.

To Jamie, my first, best friend and for your words of encouragement every day.

To Lori, for listening and reading every word, and then reading and listening again and again. I can't imagine walking through this life without you.

To Fiona, your tenderness and friendship has always been a beacon for me in my darkest times. Thank you for scooping me up and traveling with me when I sorely needed escapes.

To Mary, for just being you, which is always enough.

To Marsh, our history is our rock. Thank you for loving our Max.

To Amy, for rebalancing me. It really works.

To my OG book club ladies and Eakin moms, Tania, Cameron, Jessica, Laura, Stephenie, Carolyn, Joelle, Louise, Lynn, Lori, Chris, and Maria, even though we haven't read a book together in years, I love you all. You and your children are my touchstone to Max's childhood. Thank you.

To my BLVD gals, Anna, Hedy, Kay, Bonnie, Mary, Carolyn, Stephanie, Katy, Renata, Lisa, Kristine, Lynne, and Gini. From the moment we started gathering on Fridays to talk politics to the formation of WTF and through everything that came next—your deep and abiding friendships are what got me through it all. I love you. Catherine, we miss you.

To Katie and Molly and Dave, lifelong teenage friendships are the best.

To Heidi and Dan, Max's love lives on in you.

To the M's, who gifted me with adventures and friendships. Take credit for everything.

To Joe and Judy, who gave me a soft place to land when I left office and reminded me that there is still love and good in the world.

To Jodi, who gave up her seat and showered me with a thousand kindnesses. Thank you.

To all my classmates at Gotham and my amazing teacher, Stacy Pershall, thank you for your continued encouragement.

To everyone who has made a mistake and lost someone they love, who sent me a note, offered a word of encouragement, or stopped and hugged me at the grocery store, thank you. You lifted my spirits on days when I was struggling.

If you're still reading, thank you from the bottom of my heart for being here.

Don't forget to vote.

Megan Barry lives with her husband, Bruce, in Nashville, Tennessee.
They share their home with two rescue dogs,
Winslow, AZ and Natasha.